Elements in Indo-Pacific Security
edited by
Kai He
Griffith University
Steve Chan
University of Colorado Boulder
Rumi Aoyama
Waseda University

TAIWAN AND THE DANGER OF A SINO-AMERICAN WAR

Steve Chan
University of Colorado Boulder

Shaftesbury Road, Cambridge CB2 8EA, United Kingdom

One Liberty Plaza, 20th Floor, New York, NY 10006, USA

477 Williamstown Road, Port Melbourne, VIC 3207, Australia

314–321, 3rd Floor, Plot 3, Splendor Forum, Jasola District Centre, New Delhi – 110025, India

103 Penang Road, #05–06/07, Visioncrest Commercial, Singapore 238467

Cambridge University Press is part of Cambridge University Press & Assessment, a department of the University of Cambridge.

We share the University's mission to contribute to society through the pursuit of education, learning and research at the highest international levels of excellence.

www.cambridge.org
Information on this title: www.cambridge.org/9781009589567

DOI: 10.1017/9781009589543

© Steve Chan 2024

This publication is in copyright. Subject to statutory exception and to the provisions of relevant collective licensing agreements, no reproduction of any part may take place without the written permission of Cambridge University Press & Assessment.

When citing this work, please include a reference to the DOI 10.1017/9781009589543

First published 2024

A catalogue record for this publication is available from the British Library

ISBN 978-1-009-58956-7 Hardback
ISBN 978-1-009-58958-1 Paperback
ISSN 3033-4837 (online)
ISSN 3033-4829 (print)

Cambridge University Press & Assessment has no responsibility for the persistence or accuracy of URLs for external or third-party internet websites referred to in this publication and does not guarantee that any content on such websites is, or will remain, accurate or appropriate.

Taiwan and the Danger of a Sino-American War

Elements in Indo-Pacific Security

DOI: 10.1017/9781009589543
First published online: December 2024

Steve Chan
University of Colorado Boulder

Author for correspondence: Steve Chan, steve.chan@colorado.edu

Abstract: The author presents contrarian arguments contesting mainstream U.S. views on the danger of a Sino-American war over Taiwan's status. They contend that these countries' dispute about Taiwan is motivated by opposing strategic interests and security concerns rather than just, or even mainly, clashing values such as national reunification, sovereignty, democracy, and self-determination. The danger of a Sino-American confrontation has become more elevated recently due to a confluence of several concurrent developments. Despite this increased danger compared to any time since Richard Nixon visited Beijing in 1972, they conclude that war is not imminent or likely – barring extreme hardliners and radical nationalists taking over policymaking in Beijing, Taipei, and/or Washington. Despite a rising chorus urging Washington to commit more firmly to Taiwan's defense, they argue that the United States will not likely intervene directly on Taiwan's behalf. Even more controversially, they submit that Beijing will eventually prevail in this dispute.

Keywords: Taiwan, Sino-American War, extended deterrence, prospect theory, attribution theory

© Steve Chan 2024

ISBNs: 9781009589567 (HB), 9781009589581 (PB), 9781009589543 (OC)
ISSNs: 3033-4837 (online), 3033-4829 (print)

Contents

1 Introduction: My Main Arguments and Historical
and Theoretical Perspectives   1

2 A Perfect Storm? A Confluence of Ominous Developments   15

3 Reasons Why Neither China Nor the United States Would
Let Go of Taiwan   26

4 Strategic Ambiguity, Moral Hazard, and Prudent Statecraft   34

5 Power Balance, Effort Mobilization, and the Long Game   38

6 Conclusion: The Danger of Overreach and Self-Entrapment   43

References   54

1 Introduction: My Main Arguments and Historical and Theoretical Perspectives

Even a casual follower of recent news cycles would have noticed media coverage and commentaries on the danger of a possible crisis over Taiwan, presenting a fuse that could ignite a larger conflagration involving China and the United States. Just to introduce one example, Fareed Zakaria, a well-known host of the CNN's (Cable News Network) weekly Sunday program, GPS (Global Public Square), has written recently an opinion piece entitled "The World's Most Dangerous Place Has Only Gotten Even More Dangerous." He was referring to Taiwan (Zakaria, 2024). There has clearly been an emergent consensus in the United States on a policy of "getting tough" on China, with some former officials, academics, and media pundits calling for a revision of the existing U.S. policy to pledge publicly support for Taiwan in a military contingency involving this island. In China, there are also more strident voices demanding stronger opposition to Washington and a more hardline policy toward Taiwan. To borrow from the popular television series *Game of Thrones*, "winter is here."

I have been motivated to write this Element because of this concern. My views on this topic are in several important respects contrary to the dominant narrative on the potential danger that a dispute over Taiwan's status can escalate into a major regional and even global conflict. The original version of this Element features a long and awkward title. It is "Taiwan: Why China – and the United States – Won't Let Go, and Why the Danger of U.S. Intervention May Have Been Exaggerated and Why Beijing May Eventually Prevail." I have replaced this cumbersome title, although it does have the virtue of encapsulating the main topics that I intend to discuss and the conclusions I will draw from the following analysis.

I get concerned when, as one veteran Wall Streeter reportedly put it, "people crowd to one side of the boat." Groupthink and political conformity have been at least partially responsible for various U.S. policy fiascoes in the past with the Bay of Pigs invasion of Cuba, strategic surprise caused by Japan's Pearl Harbor attack, and China's intervention in the Korean War among its prime exhibits (Janis, 1982). If I appear to be too outspoken and strident in stating my views in the following discussion, it is because dissident voices are often not heard and even on those rare occasions when they are heard, they are not taken seriously to motivate a serious debate. In asking, "How Could Vietnam Happen?" James Thomson (1973) referred to "the domestication of dissent" to describe this phenomenon and pointed to it as one of the reasons for U.S. policy failure in that conflict.

Many of the ideas and arguments presented below have appeared originally in my recent research on Sino-American relations in general, research in which

Taiwan has received special attention because this island's contested status can be a fuse leading to a Sino-American clash. Some of this research has already been published and others were undergoing the review process (Chan, 2021, 2021, 2022a, 2023a, 2024, forthcoming/a, forthcoming/b, forthcoming/c; Chan & Hu, 2025, forthcoming/a, forthcoming/b). This is, however, the first time that I have tried to put the ideas and arguments I have presented in different studies into a more coherent and larger picture, focusing on the danger of a Sino-American war over Taiwan as a topic in its own right. Naturally, I have also introduced new material to the following discussion. Moreover, I have altered some of my earlier views in light of several recent developments, including the ongoing Russo-Ukrainian War.

This Element's main proposition is that Taiwan's contested status reflects conflicting geostrategic interests, and thus the disagreement between China and the United States on this issue is more than a clash of ideas or values. Emotions such as anger and anxiety over felt grievances and ongoing power shifts certainly play a role in the recent increase in tension between these two countries, but I argue that the main reason behind their dispute has more to do with hard-nosed calculations of *Realpolitik*. These calculations include not only geostrategic concerns of *Außenpolitik* but also considerations of *Innenpolitik* pertaining to politicians' (on all three sides, Beijing, Washington and Taipei) domestic legitimacy and their political standing. The short answer to the question "Why both China and the United States 'won't let go' of Taiwan?" is that this island impinges on their important geostrategic interests and because policies regarding this island can affect politicians' legitimacy and thus their grip on domestic power. These reasons are certainly palpable and real for China and Taiwan, but they also apply to the United States albeit to a lesser extent. To anticipate my main conclusion, notwithstanding these external and internal motivations that drive and sustain dispute over Taiwan's status, a Sino-American war is in my view unlikely – which is of course different from saying that it is impossible.

What do I mean when I say neither China nor the United States "would let go" of Taiwan? I have in mind simply the idea that Beijing will not quit its claim of sovereignty over Taiwan. In its 1972 joint communique with Beijing (Taiwan Documents Project, no date), Washington had "acknowledged" that Beijing represents the legitimate government of China and that Chinese on both sides of the Taiwan Strait see this island as part of China. But its actual policy has sought to support this island's continued separation from China. There is continuity in this policy since at least the outbreak of the Korean War, when Harry Truman ordered the Seventh Fleet to "neutralize" the Taiwan Strait, thus frustrating the Beijing government's plan to take over this last bastion of the Kuomintang or

Taiwan and the Danger of a Sino-American War

the Nationalists, who were defeated in the civil war on the Chinese mainland. Washington's opposition to any attempt by Beijing to resort to force to resolve Taiwan's status has the practical effect of sustaining this island's *de facto* independence. The United States is unlikely to abandon this position in the foreseeable future – if anything, some people are urging Washington to strengthen its support for Taipei. Thus, "not letting go" means that the United States is unlikely to disassociate itself from the controversy over Taiwan's status, leaving Taipei to face China alone. All three parties – Taipei, Beijing, and Washington – know that the United States is the main obstacle standing in the way of China's goal of national reunification. As long as Washington "has its back," Taipei is likely to hold out against Beijing's pressure for reunification or at least to resist Beijing's terms for settlement.

Implied in my remarks just now are two propositions. First, all parties to this dispute know each other's intentions well. I would even submit that they also have a good understanding of one another's concerns, fears, and redlines. To a large extent, one can attribute the peace and stability that have thus far prevailed across the Taiwan Strait to this mutual understanding since Richard Nixon visited Beijing in 1972. Iain Johnston (2011: 28) has remarked that "there is evidence that the very top levels of both sides [China and the United States] actually have a better understanding of each other's interests and red lines than is implied in public debates." Although I agree with this view, I do not have any direct evidence to prove it. My remark about leaders of all three sides knowing one another well should therefore be seen more in the context of my argument that the idea of security dilemma has been overused and that studies of at least some past conflicts have shown that wars are not always the result of blunders but can also happen because of deliberate choice.

Second, the relevant parties' intentions – reflecting their respective motivations and calculations – are unlikely to change barring some major unexpected developments. In other words, the current impasse is likely to continue. Taiwan's strategic location impinges on China's tangible security interests, and it is conversely important for U.S. efforts to contain China. The dispute over its status thus involves more than just its symbolic value to the Chinese aspiration of national reunification. Of course, the latter motivation is not irrelevant. James Fearon (1995) has argued that incompatible interests and discrepant expectations of their relative performance on the battlefield can cause states to fight despite war's known inefficiency. In the case of Taiwan, sovereignty involves an "indivisible good" (Goddard, 2006), thus compounding further the disputants' difficulty to reach a settlement to avoid war.

How stable is this impasse? That is, what can possibly upset the current situation perhaps best described as "cold peace"? This is another way of asking what might undermine, shatter, and even displace the established views and understandings that I have attributed to the leaders of all three sides. Framed in this way, disruptive domestic politics that empower a hawkish counterelite are the most likely source of this threat. When the politics of demagoguery, nationalism and populism gain a large influence in or even take over the policymaking process, all analytic bets are off.

Powerful particularistic interests and domestic lobbies, such as the iron-and-rye coalition in Wilhelmine Germany, have in the past captured the commanding heights of state policymaking and hijacked the national agenda. Some people, such as orthodox Marxists, who see the capitalist state as the bourgeoisie's executive committee, may look askance at this remark, but I would argue that the nature of the ruling coalition makes a huge difference in a state's policy agenda and direction (e.g., Snyder, 1993; Solingen, 2007). Although limited space will not allow me to delve into details about domestic politics, I see the United States undergoing a political transformation that has shattered its previous consensus on foreign policy and heightened its political discord and cultural divisiveness. Donald Trump's "Make American Great Again" movement has already changed profoundly political discourse and partisan balance in the United States. Regardless of whether he wins the next presidential term, there is likely to be more turmoil and uncertainty in U.S. foreign policymaking. Judged by the statements of former Trump appointees or associates such as Steve Bannon, Mike Pompeo, and John Bolton, Sino-American relations may be taken to a more confrontational direction if they or others like them were to be put in positions responsible for making U.S. foreign policy. They are in my opinion the more likely and capable "disruptors" or "revisionists" who can overturn the status quo.

Ongoing social, economic, and political change in China, Taiwan, and the United States can alter their respective *domestic* balance of political influence and interests and thus upend the mutual understanding and reciprocal accommodation that have thus far kept their disagreements from escalating into an armed showdown. These changes appear more palpable in the United States recently. Chinese nationalism has always been a factor in Beijing's foreign policy, and it can be exploited and manipulated by the elite. However, those factors that are usually invoked in U.S. narratives of China's bellicosity – such as its authoritarian government, its communist ideology, and its populist and nationalist tendencies – are, relatively speaking, constants, and as constants they cannot explain change suggesting more strained Sino-American relations.

Authoritarian leaders may be in a better position to rein in mass sentiments favoring bellicosity. Competing elites in democracies can be expected to appeal to and mobilize such sentiments for partisan gains – although this can also surely happen in China. This being the case, the emergence of elite division and competition in Beijing can be an important sign that political instability and policy change may be afoot. My view goes against the grain of analyses decrying Xi Jinping's consolidation of power, but it follows from Robert Putnam's (1988) logic of two-level games, suggesting that authoritarian leaders – or more generally, leaders who are secure in their political control and domestic power – are in a stronger position to compromise in enabling a deal with their foreign counterparts. Authoritarian leaders face a smaller selectorate (Bueno de Mesquita & Smith 2012; Bueno de Mesquita et al., 2003), fewer veto groups, and greater policy space or a wider negotiation range because of their lower bar for domestic ratification of this deal.

The danger of a clash over the Taiwan Strait has increased recently – primarily because of domestic political changes occurring in Taiwan and the United States. As discussed later, ongoing power shifts between China and the United States have also contributed to tension and anxiety. If not necessarily auguring a greater danger of war, the breakdown of the traditional bipartisan consensus of liberal internationalism in the United States (Kupchan & Trubowitz, 2007, 2010, 2021a, 2021b) suggests greater discord and uncertainty in Washington's formulation and conduct of its foreign policy.

The discussion below explains why in my view the danger of a Sino-American confrontation over Taiwan has increased. This proposition, however, only compares the current situation with that which has prevailed since 1972. It does *not* argue that a Sino-American clash is imminent or inevitable. I agree with Scott Kastner (2022) that we should not exaggerate this danger. Compared to much of recent discourse in the United States, this is a relatively sanguine view based on my proposition that the leaders of all three sides of the Taiwan dispute have a good understanding of one another's motivations and calculations – assuming that they are not overtaken or overpowered by hot heads and jingoists. Washington has acted quite prudently in previous situations that might have put it on a collision course with Moscow or Beijing.

The other part of my relatively sanguine view that war over Taiwan's status is unlikely reflects my inference of Beijing's calculus, especially its belief that time is on China's side. Of course, Chinese leaders have warned that their patience is not infinite, and the resolution of Taiwan's status cannot be deferred forever from generation to generation. Still, I believe that they clearly understand that even if they prevail in a military campaign to seize Taiwan, it will be a pyrrhic victory – with enormous damage to the island's infrastructure, China's agenda for economic development, and its aspirations for global ascendance. China has already made relative gains in closing the military gap between it and the United States. It has also already waited some seventy-five years to reunify

6   *Indo-Pacific Security*

with Taiwan. Although the prospects for a peaceful reunification have dimmed for the near future as I discuss below, I am also inclined to believe that Beijing's leaders will take a long-term view suggesting that with the passage of time, their bargaining position relative to Washington and Taipei will improve. Hence, I am not quite inclined to accept dire warnings circulating in some quarters, predicting that Beijing will start a military campaign against Taiwan in the next three, five, or ten years.

A strong implication follows from my argument that the dispute over Taiwan's status impinges on tangible political and security interests for both Beijing and Washington. It is that the leaders of these countries are not chasing after some imaginary or "phantom" reasons that motivate their contest. Or, in other words, the Sino-American dispute over Taiwan's status is not *just* due to some ideational construct, such as national reunification for China and defense of democracy for the United States – at least not only, or even mainly, for these reasons in my view. This remark of course does not suggest that ideas and norms are irrelevant or unimportant; it only argues that they should not be exaggerated. Although these reasons are often stressed by respected scholars and also less serious media commentators and pundits, I question their relative weight in explaining the conduct of the parties involved in the dispute over Taiwan's status.

Another implication of the following discussion is that contrary again to prevailing thinking, even that which is reflected in serious and erudite scholarship, should war occur between China and the United States over Taiwan's status, it would not necessarily or even primarily be due to some tragic misperception or miscalculation. As already mentioned, domestic factors can produce a confrontation. Some wars have happened in the past even under conditions that approximate the rational, unitary actor model (Allison, 1971). In other words, wars sometimes happen not because leaders stumbled into them but rather because they had deliberately sought them. Germany's leaders went to war in 1914 with their eyes wide open (e.g., Lieber, 2007), and Japanese leaders acted likewise in deciding to attack Pearl Harbor – even though they realized that their country was eight or nine times weaker than the United States and that they were taking a huge gamble that could end very badly for their country (e.g., Ike, 1967; Russett, 1969). Similarly, the administration of George W. Bush invaded Iraq *not* because some regrettable failure in intelligence suggesting that Saddam Hussein had (or was developing) weapons of mass destruction and that he had affiliations or connections with Al Qaeda (which had committed the 9/11 attacks on the United States).

Not to put too fine a point on it, people in Moscow, Beijing, and many other capitals including U.S. allies believe that the public reasons presented by the

Bush administration to invade Iraq were bogus – lies contrived to justify its "preventive war." Even some Americans believe that in this case, there was a spectacular failure in the marketplace of ideas and in the functioning of democratic institutions such as on the part of Congress and the media to enable – indeed, to support – the Bush administration's rush to unleash an unnecessary war (to borrow from the title of a well-known article by Mearsheimer and Walt published in 2003 before the United States invaded Iraq), a war that it was already inclined to undertake before 9/11 (Kaufman, 2004; Mazarr, 2007). China and Russia were deeply disturbed and seriously concerned by various other examples of assertive U.S. unilateralism, including its attacks on Serbia and Libya. Even Americans have written about this assertive unilateralism and Washington's revisionist agenda in promoting color revolutions and pushing for regime changes abroad (e.g., Daalder & Lindsay, 2005; Walt, 2005).

My main point in making these remarks is that the so-called security dilemma (Jervis, 1978) has been overused in explanations of international conflicts, including in the case of a possible war between the United States and China due to a contingency involving Taiwan. The idea of security dilemma of course argues that international conflicts happen because, tragically, both sides of a dispute misinterpret the other party's defensive actions to mean offensive intention, leading to a spiral of suspicion and antagonism. The resulting momentum of escalating tit-for-tat eventually results in war – such as in Lewis Richardson's (1960) famous model of armament race suggesting what can happen *if* leaders react to their counterpart's moves mechanistically, that is, *unthinkingly.*

I believe that if a Sino-American conflict over Taiwan happens, it would not be the result of security dilemma as just described. Instead, as already stated I tend to see the top leaders in Beijing, Washington, and Taipei to be realistic and rational individuals. Moreover, they actually know one another's views, concerns, and redlines quite well – well enough to know which button to push to irritate the hell out the other party but also to pull back before crossing this counterpart's bottom line. Again, this view does not deny that emotions can play a role in these officials' formulations and conduct of their countries' foreign policy, and it of course also does not remove the possibility of misunderstanding or misperception. "Hot button" issues and emotionally charged disputes obviously reflect historical experiences and political construction.

Constructivists are right in pointing out "anarchy" and other ideas such as "sovereignty" and "nationality" are ideational constructs (Wendt, 1992). Moreover, settling grudges and pursuing status (e.g., Larson & Shevchenko, 2010, 2019; Lebow, 2010; Murray, 2010, 2019; Renshon, 2016, 2017; Ward, 2017) certainly also influence interstate conflicts. John Vasquez (2009: 133, italic in original) has remarked that "war and violence occur because of *grievances* and not just power." Thus, I would certainly not deny or dismiss the role of emotions in politics. Yet, disputes can also happen because of a real clash of tangible interests. Naturally, domestic "push" and external "pull" (by allies) can also get countries into a war (Welch, 2015, 2020). In this study, I give analytic priority to rationalist explanations. These explanations and those based on constructivist interpretations are not mutually exclusive. Social scientists should keep in mind the idea of equifinality – meaning that different causal paths can lead to the same outcome. These paths are also not mutually exclusive.

Besides World War I, the Cuban Missile Crisis, and the U.S. invasion of Iraq, I can think of many other episodes such as North Korea's attack on South Korea, the subsequent U.S. intervention and Chinese counter-intervention in that conflict, and the Yom Kippur War as instances when leaders have knowingly started or gone to war. The subsequent conflict might not have turned out as they had planned or hoped for, such as for the United States in Vietnam, Iraq, and Afghanistan, but this does not mean that they had not chosen war consciously.

One empirical pattern seems to lend indirect support to my contention. The recurrence of armed conflicts between so-called enduring rivals accounts for a disproportionately large number of military conflicts in history (Chan, 2024b; Diehl, 1998; Diehl & Goertz, 2000; Thompson, 1995). Even though these pairs of disputatious states constitute only a tiny minority of all possible dyads in the world, they are recidivists that get into militarized disputes and armed conflicts time and again far in excess of the rest of interstate community. This phenomenon would be puzzling for those who argue that leaders tend to blunder into war because compared to the other dyads, officials of these enduring rivals – often close neighbors sharing cultural affinity and extensive experience in dealing with each other (e.g., North and South Korea, India and Pakistan, Israel and its Arab neighbors, Ukraine and Russia, and, of course, China and Taiwan) – should be most familiar with the concerns, motivations, and calculations of their respective counterparts and should therefore be least prone to commit the errors of misperception or misunderstanding. After all, they are serial disputants who should have gotten to know each other well from their many prior encounters.

Lest I get too far ahead of myself, let me now take a step back to sketch how the remainder of the Element will unfold and to offer a preview of my arguments. In Section 2, I will explain in general terms why ongoing trends have made a clash between China and the United States over Taiwan now and in the near future more likely than at any other time since their rapprochement when Richard Nixon visited Beijing in 1972. I will show that the escalating danger of

Taiwan and the Danger of a Sino-American War 9

a war over Taiwan is not somebody's figment of imagination and that it has become an increasing concern for U.S. officials.

I will introduce public warnings by top U.S. military officers that this conflict can happen even in the next three years, as well as secret phone calls made by top U.S. brass General Mark Milley to reassure his Chinese counterpart that the United States was not planning to launch a surprise attack on China. In addition, I will introduce statements made by Chinese and U.S. leaders to show that they too believe that there is a palpable danger of a war between their countries happening over Taiwan. I will report statements by Deng Xiaoping and Xi Jinping to show the importance that Beijing attaches to Taiwan's status and these Chinese leaders' perception of the role played by the United States in the impasse on this issue over the past seventy-five years, and also commitments made by various U.S. leaders, including recent remarks by Joe Biden on Washington's intention to defend its allies. I will also refer briefly to the ongoing debate in Washington about whether to abandon its policy of strategic ambiguity and to replace it with an outright public pledge to defend Taiwan.

In Section 3, I will get on with trying to answer the main question taken up in this Element. Why neither China nor the United States would "let go" of Taiwan? I argue that the usual cliché about Chinese nationalism and communism is way too facile and indeed misleading, and I will try to show why Taiwan is important for China's national security and its leaders' domestic legitimacy and their hold on power. I also question the usual trope about Washington's commitment to defend freedom, democracy, and the right to self-determination. I introduce U.S. relations with Cuba, which provides the closest parallel to that of China's relations with Taiwan. The typical reasons featured in explanations often advanced by U.S. scholars and pundits about China's ostensible aggressiveness are not persuasive in part because I strongly suspect that they would not accept the same logic and reasons (Chinese nationalism and communism) as an explanation of U.S. conduct toward Cuba. In my view, Washington's support for many authoritarian regimes and its opposition to secession movements on the grounds of self-determination currently and in the past render its claims about Taiwan not believable. They may be useful for mobilizing domestic support, but they will be unconvincing to the rest of the world and neutral observers.

Frankly, I see the prevailing U.S. discourse on Taiwan to be – yes, political construction, and not necessarily in the usual sense of ideational constructs and the development of enemy images (e.g., Oren, 2003; Rousseau, 2006) although that is involved too, but rather more in the context of political entrepreneurship to promote a policy agenda, to frame a policy question, to influence public and elite opinion, and to mobilize support for a preferred policy as in the discussion by Frank Baumgartner and Bryan Jones ([1993] 2009) on policymaking in general, and as in the analyses of a hegemon's ideational or structural power by Antonio Gramsci (1971), Steven Lukes (1975), and Michael Barnett and Raymond Duvall (2005). Or, if you will, recent U.S. discourse on the need to "get tough" toward China is a "solution" chasing after a "problem" as in the "garbage can" model of policymaking presented by Cohen et al. (1972). Recall that it was not so long ago that Washington had claimed that the government in Taipei was the legitimate representative of China – all of China, including the mainland – and was thus entitled to the China seat in the United Nations. It has since made a U-turn in its policy, claiming that Beijing does not represent the people of Taiwan even though, as already remarked, it has "acknowledged" Taiwan being part of China in its joint communique with Beijing.

Americans appear to have a national amnesia about how they had settled their own civil war – by bullets, not ballots. Barry Buzan and Robert Cox (2023: 118) wrote forthrightly, "Parallels could in fact be drawn between the ruthless military anti-secession and rejection of self-determination that underpinned the US civil war, and China's similar current attitudes towards Tibet, Taiwan, and Xinjiang. Abraham Lincoln and the Chinese Communist Party would perhaps have understood each other quite well on this question." There is a reason why Lincoln is held in such esteem by Americans nowadays (although not while he was alive), and that reason pertains to his determination to preserve the Union and resist the South's attempt to secede. Why should it be different for Xi?

Many Americans would be horrified by this comparison, and their reaction would not be unique. Many Chinese would also be astounded by Buzan and Cox's reference to Tibet, Taiwan, and Xinjiang. Introspection is not a trait for most people. Americans and Chinese are not alone to overlook their respective country's checkered history. The British, for example, condemn China's conduct toward Taiwan and in Xinjiang as if for many of them the history of their brutal suppression of the Irish independence movement and, more recently, Kenyan resistance to their colonial rule – for which, credit to him, King Charles has at least expressed "regret" – had never happened. They often criticize China's abuse of human rights even though it was not so long ago when they opposed strongly sanctions against South Africa's apartheid and Rhodesia's racist government.

After explaining that Taiwan is important for China's national security and the serious domestic fallout for any Chinese leader who is seen to be weak on Taiwan, thus seriously jeopardizing his/her domestic legitimacy and hold on power, I will turn in Section 4 to discuss why Washington's heretofore policy of strategic ambiguity toward Taiwan and China is unconvincing. I will also argue

Taiwan and the Danger of a Sino-American War 11

that it had acted with great caution and restraint in past situations involving the danger of a direct clash with the USSR/Russia or China. The thrust of this discussion is that the probability of a U.S. military intervention in a crisis involving Taiwan is actually smaller than often implied in current popular U.S. narratives on this topic. These narratives are often in my view distorted, simplistic, sensational, and based on little knowledge about China and Taiwan – and as just suggested, even the history of the United States itself.

I contend that leaders in Washington are not unaware of the true nature of the Taiwan problem. There are good reasons for them to adopt a policy of strategic ambiguity so that they would not back themselves into a corner or create a moral hazard (Benson, 2012). There was a time when Washington had wanted to "leash" Chiang Kai-shek, and some scholars have suggested that the primary reason for its security treaty with Taiwan and South Korea reflected the adage that alliances are created *not* simply or even primarily for the accretion of power but rather also and even mainly for reasons that led Paul Schroeder (1976) to call them *pacta de contrahendo,* or pacts of restraint (see also Snyder, 1997). Given its overwhelming power, the United States certainly did not need support from small partners such as Taiwan during the Cold War. Indeed, the very definition of a superpower is that it is not dependent on the rest of its alliance to compete with its counterpart superpower.

Rather, alliances are often designed to serve the more powerful country's objective of controlling an unruly junior partner, lest its protégé such as Taiwan or South Korea (under Syngman Rhee) "trap" it in an unwanted war (Benson, 2012; Kim, 2019; Murata, 2007). Britain did not commit itself definitely to fight on France's behalf in the lead-up to World War I in part because London was concerned about the danger of Paris taking advantage of this support to provoke Germany – with the tragic consequence that Berlin entertained the false hope that Britain might remain neutral until just before war broke out.

Another perverse consequence of moral hazard stemming from a firm commitment to defend a protégé can be to abet this junior partner's incentive to free ride (Olson, 1965; Olson & Zeckhauser, 1966). Why should it pay for its own defense, when its larger and more powerful sponsor or ally can be expected to take on this burden? Indeed, David Kang (2023) has shown that until the last few years, Taiwan's military spending has been stagnating and even declining. Its defense spending as a percentage of GDP (gross domestic product) was 2.04% in 2010, 1.87% in 2015, and 1.74% in 2021. This defense burden *declined* 0.29% between 2010 and 2021 and 0.12% between 2015 and 2021. Naturally, this phenomenon is an anomaly from the realist perspective, which expects states to undertake "internal balancing" against a hostile neighbor growing stronger (in the terminology of Kenneth Waltz's influential book published in 1979, internal balancing refers to a state's own efforts to develop its military capabilities, whereas external balancing refers to its search for allies to jointly oppose another country).

Plausible reasons for this seemingly puzzling behavior on the part of Taiwan could be that it does not expect China to attack, that it believes the United States has its back, that it has higher priorities such as domestic welfare and economic growth, that it faces strong domestic opposition to increasing defense spending, or a combination of these and other considerations. Its behavior may even reflect its belief that it is a fool's errand to get into an arms' race against its much larger neighbor, a fatal mistake made by the Kremlin that drove the USSR into financial insolvency, economic decline, and eventually political disintegration and regime collapse. I will refrain from further discussion of Taiwan's seeming enigmatic behavior in this regard as it will require another extended study.

For reasons explained by James Fearon (1994, 1997), extended deterrence involves a binary choice of committing to defend a protégé or not. Thus, a policy of strategic ambiguity is inherently not credible. It is also not absolutely clear that the ongoing debate in Washington about abandoning this policy of strategic ambiguity in favor of a firm commitment to defend Taiwan actually indicates a change in its intention (a possibility that would cause alarm in Beijing) – or just a head fake to deliberately heighten U.S. deterrence threat without actually publicizing so officially and thereby committing Washington's reputation formally to a new policy and limiting its future discretion. As I will argue later, Washington has in fact acted prudently in past situations involving the risk of a direct clash with the USSR/Russia or China.

As Fearon has reminded us, officials and politicians often engage in strategic posturing or what he calls "misrepresentation." They may deliberately exaggerate their stake or resolve in a dispute in attempting to convince their counterpart to make concessions. This remark is not inconsistent with the observation that the two opposing sides in a dispute may also have real and even serious differences of interest; it only contends that they can try to inflate their determination to stand their ground or have their way in order to gain a bargaining advantage. When a country has an obvious interest in a dispute – such as China in the case of Taiwan – it does not need to bluff because others will understand its evident stake. Conversely, when it obviously does not have a stake in a dispute, bluffing will be useless and even counterproductive as others would call its bluff. It is in the intermediate range of a state's interest or stake in a dispute that bluffing is most likely. Moreover, weak states are reluctant to bluff because they are afraid of having their bluff called and the consequences that would follow. Strong states have a greater incentive to bluff because they know that others are wary of calling their bluff even when they suspect it. Weaker states are wary to call a stronger state's bluff because of the possibility of severe consequences should they be mistaken (Sartori, 2005). The implications of this discussion should be evident for China and the United States. A country can present an aggressive posture without, however, following up on its threats.

In Section 5, I argue that most of the prevailing academic discussion on the danger of a Sino-American war over Taiwan has a misplaced emphasis, namely being excessively concerned with the shifting balance of military capabilities across the Taiwan Strait and between China and the United States. Of course, shifting power balance, including military capabilities, matters, but I argue that the outcomes of war are influenced not just by raw power. If this were the case, the United States would have prevailed in its wars in Korea, Vietnam, Iraq, and Afghanistan. The outcomes of war are also determined by the relative resolve of the contestants, their relative stake in the dispute, and their willingness to endure hardship and suffer privations. Moreover, wars involve a contest of stamina and perseverance – a long game dependent on the belligerents' dedication to their cause. In short, wars are also a contest of will, and not just one of power. I argue that the basic asymmetries in the amount of stake for each country and therefore their relative resolve to stand their ground imply that the United States may not be as likely to involve itself in an armed confrontation with China as one may infer from some of the current commentaries and analyses. Better not get into a morass only to pull back subsequently after shedding a large amount of blood, sweat, and tears – not to mention also the expenditure of dollars and political capital.

Just like the United States, China has acted cautiously in previous crisis situations involving the United States. It has also been patient, having put off forcing a definitive settlement of the Taiwan issue for seventy-five years now. Although one sometimes hears from both Americans and Chinese that China is done with biding its time, I believe that Chinese leaders are still adhering to Deng Xiaoping's admonition that China should bide its time and hide its brilliance (韜光養晦). The bottom line in my view is that contestation over Taiwan involves a long game, a Marathon, and a test of endurance. What will happen in ten, twenty, or fifty years from now? We can be reasonably sure that Beijing will still care about Taiwan. Will the United States and if so, to what extent? Who is going to outwait whom? Naturally, recent trends and likely future trajectories in power shifts between these disputants also matter. Despite the idea popular in some quarters that China is losing its patience, I would rather tend to think that as a rising state (albeit growing at a much slower pace in the coming years compared to previous decades), its leaders will continue to let "the trend be their friend" – that is, to wait out the current turbulence roiling their country's relationship with the United States. If this view is correct, it implies that the United States is likely to be more impatient as its window of opportunity to coerce China may be closing in the next decade or two (on whether leaders "jump" through these "windows," see Lebow, 1984).

Section 6 summarizes my conclusions which contain large elements of conjecture although I try to be explicit about my logic and rationale. Nevertheless, my conclusions can be controversial such as in suggesting, as implied by the remark at the end of the last paragraph, that it is the United States that is more likely to act aggressively in the immediate future than China – and also that in the end Washington will probably decide *not* to intervene militarily in a conflict across the Taiwan Strait. These two views may appear paradoxical, but they are not contradictory. Those advocating that Washington should commit itself to Taiwan's defense evidently believe that the United States still has the military upper hand vis-à-vis China, although it is unclear how long they expect this situation to last. It seems also obvious that the proponents for "strategic clarity" to replace Washington's heretofore policy of "strategic ambiguity" believe that a more definite announcement of U.S. intention to defend Taiwan can be used to offset China's recent (relative) gains that have closed the military gap separating it from the United States. However, words are not enough; such declarations have to be made credible by costly action without which they are likely to be dismissed as hot air (Fearon, 1997).

In conclusion, both China and the United States are in my view clear-eyed, cool-headed rational actors, and if past experience is any guide, neither is likely to be swayed by emotional outbursts. Whether they decide to go to war will be based on their hard-nosed calculations of their strategic interests and stakes – compared to the costs and risks involved in fighting. This view in turn causes me to be relatively sanguine about the prospect that they will be able to avoid an armed conflict. Of course, the danger of miscalculation always exists, but I tend to believe that the top leaders of both countries actually have a good understanding of their counterparts' fears, concerns, and redlines. The United States has of course fought in various countries such as Korea, Vietnam, Iraq, and Afghanistan. But China is none of these. In the past – even at the height of the Cuban Missile Crisis in 1962, a conflict occurring in the U.S. backyard, where it had an overwhelming conventional advantage and when it also had a commanding nuclear edge – Washington had acted prudently. The "wild card" in my view is, as already mentioned, if hotheads and political demagogues in either country seize power and precipitate and escalate a confrontation.

My conclusions can be controversial. Other people can, for example, disagree with my proposition that the United States will in the end refrain from intervening on behalf of Taiwan and my contention that Beijing will eventually prevail

Taiwan and the Danger of a Sino-American War 15

in the current impasse over this island's status. The concluding section also emphasizes two important points about overreach and self-entrapment. They refer to self-inflicted injuries due to overcommitments abroad beyond available means and exaggerated rhetoric damaging a country's reputation for credibility and reliability. Both can have serious long-term deleterious consequences. Their relevance naturally extends beyond the immediate case pertaining to a crisis over Taiwan. If this Element encourages an open and full-throated debate on these and other related issues, it would have served its purpose.

2 A Perfect Storm? A Confluence of Ominous Developments

Several concurrent trends have converged to elevate the danger of a war over Taiwan. Some of these trends pertain more specifically to conditions in Taiwan and China, while others concern more generally the relationship between the United States and China. Each of these ongoing developments contributes to tension, but the combined effect of their interactions is more concerning than their separate influence individually on the rising danger of a conflagration.

Although over the past three or so decades Taiwan's economic relationship with China has deepened, this development has not produced a concomitant change in its people's receptivity to Beijing's campaign to reunify this island with the mainland (for a most recent analysis of Taiwan's public opinion in the wake of the Russo-Ukrainian War in February 2022, see Wang & Cheng, 2024). Chinese mainland has become Taiwan's most important trade partner and the largest destination of its outbound investment. At the same time, people in Taiwan have increasingly shifted their identity from being Chinese to being Taiwanese. The Democratic Progressive Party, which promotes the eventual goal of independence for Taiwan, has become the majority party, even though the opposition party, the Kuomintang or the Nationalist Party, continues to score some important electoral victories in local and legislative contests. Public opinion in Taiwan and the relative strength of the two main parties in Taiwan suggest that Beijing's attempts at peaceful reunification have largely failed. The majority of Taiwan's people would favor independence – absent Beijing's threat to use force in that event. In the face of this threat, the majority prefers to maintain the current situation – postponing any attempt to resolve the island's status until an indefinite future (e.g., Benson & Niou, 2005; Chan, 2021; Hsieh & Niou, 2005; Lin, 2016; Liu, 2016; Rigger, 2011; Wang, 2017, 2021; Wang & Liu, 2004; Wu, 2016; Yang, 2016).

Two implications follow from this situation. First, even though Taipei and Washington have constantly urged China to forswear the use of force, Beijing will almost certainly not do so – because it sees this threat to be the main, if not the only, reason that has deterred Taiwan from declaring independence. Second, although Taipei and Washington may accept the current situation as their second-best choice, why should Beijing accept Taiwan's *de facto* independence in perpetuity in exchange for it to eschew declaring its *de jure* independence? Beijing has stated that its patience is not infinite.

One reason for Beijing's more insistent position is that the military balance across the Taiwan Strait and that between China and the United States have shifted in its relative favor. Whereas even just two decades ago Beijing's military capabilities were quite limited, it has recently modernized its armed forces to such an extent that it can now mount a credible threat to the island and to deny U.S. access to Taiwan's vicinity. Another reason for Beijing's posture is, as just mentioned, that its "soft" approach based mainly on economic enticements has failed to persuade Taiwan's people and its politicians to reunify with China. Its hope for peaceful reunification has been diminished greatly if not entirely dashed. Having taken note of Beijing's more insistent tone and seeming impatience more recently, I will discuss later why Beijing is still likely to adopt a wait-and-see attitude because it expects further improvement in its bargaining position vis-à-vis Taiwan and the United States.

Yet another reason for the current tense situation pertains to Sino-American relations, which have served in the past as a ballast to calm occasional turbulence across the Taiwan Strait. Economic development and, at earlier times, strategic cooperation to oppose the USSR received a higher priority in Beijing. Chinese leaders have stressed the importance of maintaining a stable, if not always cordial, relationship with the United States, putting their country's economic growth at the very top of their policy agenda while setting aside the thorny issue regarding Taiwan for the time being. Now that the Cold War is over, the United States has started its economic decoupling from China, and Beijing appears no longer inclined to subordinate all of its objectives to economic growth, the situation has changed significantly.

The influence of economic interdependence on peace has been debated by scholars. Such interdependence did not prevent Britain and Germany from going to war in 1914, and there is an emergent consensus that it presents a double-edged sword (e.g., Barbieri, 2002; Copeland, 1996; Mansfield & Pollins, 2003; Russett & Oneal, 2001; Farrel & Newman, 2019; Gartzke et al., 2001). In the case of Sino-American relations, this variable's importance in restraining conflict has declined in view of Washington's recent economic coercion directed against China, such as to boycott its telecommunications companies, block technology transfers, and relocate supply chains. For both Beijing and Washington, economic considerations are subordinate to national security. China's authoritarian government, communist ideology, and abuse of human rights did not prevent Sino-American rapprochement and indeed strategic cooperation during the Nixon, Ford, and Carter administrations.

Thus, I attach less weight to these factors than strategic interests in explaining changes in Sino-American relations. As implied earlier, I interpret U.S. statements about defending Taiwan's democracy and protecting its people's self-determination and human rights as an attempt to frame popular discourse and mobilize public support. They do not appear very persuasive as alternative explanations of Washington's current policy toward Taiwan or its strained relations with Beijing. After all, Washington's support for Taiwan was the strongest when this island was ruled by an authoritarian government under martial law and its rapprochement with Beijing occurred when China's society and economy were more closed and its people's socioeconomic rights more restricted than now.

Although power-transition theory (Organski & Kugler, 1980) is flawed in several important ways, it is right in pointing to the destabilizing effects of rapid and large power shifts – which have characterized the relationship between China and the United States in recent decades (Chan, 2020, forthcoming/c). This factor and others just mentioned have undermined the heretofore seeming stability characterizing relations across the Taiwan Strait. These power shifts have in turn led to policy shifts for government officials and problem shifts for academic researchers (Chan, forthcoming/c). Although relations among all three parties (Taiwan, China, and the United States) have heretofore appeared to be calm on the surface, important changes reflecting macro trends have in fact been unfolding beneath the surface. I disagree, however, with power-transition theory's propositions that an approaching parity between two states presages conflict between them and that this conflict is likely to be initiated by a cocky upstart. I rather tend to see more merit in the traditional realist tenet that a balance of power promotes peace and stability (e.g., Waltz, 1979). I have explained my objections to power-transition theory and Thucydides' Trap (Allison, 2017) elsewhere (Chan, 2008, 2020), and will not discuss further this topic because of space limitations.

Recent macro trends unfolding in Taiwan's relations with China point to changing Taiwanese identity, the popularity of the pro-independence Democratic Progressive Party, deepening economic ties across the Taiwan Strait, rising Chinese military capabilities, and increasing schism between Beijing and Washington in the years after the Cold War's end but especially in the last several years since Donald Trump's administration started to impose tariffs on China's exports to the United States and embargo Chinese telecommunications companies such as Huawei. These policies have been continued by the Biden administration, and tension seems to have in some respects even escalated as shown by the action taken by the U.S. House of Representatives to ban TikTok unless its Chinese parent firm Byte-Dance divests its ownership stake in this social media company. Although he criticized Trump's tariffs on Chinese goods, Biden has increased them such as for Chinese electric vehicles and solar panels. China has of course not been passive in the game of tit-for-tat, although its retaliations have not generally been as strong as U.S. policies. Although there are always competing claims of "he said, she said," it is my impression that Beijing has typically assumed a more reactive role to Washington's initiatives.

China's rise has aroused concern, anxiety, and even alarm in the United States. This change is in my view the fundamental reason for Washington's turn to take a more hardline against China, which it has identified as the leading revisionist competitor posing the most serious challenge to the U.S. global leadership position. Washington had already declared its national security goal of deterring any country that would pose such a challenge over twenty years ago (e.g., White House, 2002). China has been in Washington's crosshairs ever since. Taiwan is not in itself intrinsically important to the United States, which cares about Taiwan because China cares about Taiwan. The rising danger of a Sino-American collision over Taiwan is derivative of the serious deterioration in these countries' bilateral relationship. Taiwan, in other words, is a symptom of this worsening relationship, not its cause.

Some people may argue that if China were a democracy, its rise would not be so concerning to the United States. There may be a kernel of truth in this proposition. After all, the exchange of the leadership baton between Britain and the United States was peaceful (Schake, 2017). This proposition, however, is undermined by the fact that these countries had several "close calls" whereby they almost came to exchanging blows (Bourne, 1967; Layne, 1994). Moreover, in the late 1800s and early 1900s Britain had also accommodated other rising states such as Russia and Japan (which were obviously not democracies) and it had reconciled with its historical rival France in order to concentrate its limited resources on a threat closer to its home islands, namely, Germany. The only other relevant case that comes to mind pertains to the commercial competition posed by Japan to the United States during the 1970s and 1980s. Even though Japan was a fellow democracy and even an alliance partner, there was much U.S. handwringing at that time. One only need to recall popular books at the time with titles such as *Japan as Number One* (Vogel, 1979), *Trading Places: How We Are Giving Our Future to Japan and How to Reclaim It* (Prestowitz, 1990), and even *The Coming War with Japan* (Friedman & LeBard, 1991)!

The United States is unlikely to respond to the rise of any country with equanimity, whether it is a democracy or not. That is, *Realpolitik* considerations would trump regime or ideological affinity. During the Maoist years and even during the years when Deng Xiaoping was in control of China's policies, this country's authoritarianism and its communist ideology did not stop Sino-American rapprochement and even strategic cooperation to oppose the USSR. There is no doubt that Chinese society and economy have become more open in the years since. If ideals such as a more open society, greater civil liberties, more extensive economic intercourse and other kinds of engagement with the rest of the world, stronger support for multilateral diplomacy, international organizations and arms control, complete renunciation of former Maoist support for violent insurrections abroad to overthrow foreign governments, and lastly higher living standards for the masses (an important part of human rights which includes the alleviation of poverty, hunger and diseases) were at the top of Washington's list of interests, the United States would welcome these changes by Beijing since the 1970s and congratulate itself for having played a part in promoting these changes by China. In fact, it has not (Chan, 2023a, 2023b). Indeed, quite the opposite. There is widespread talk in Washington nowadays that its policy to engage China has *failed* (e.g., Campbell & Ratner, 2018; Campbell & Sullivan, 2020; Campbell & Rapp-Hooper, 2020; Kagan, 2005)!

Reflecting this deterioration in Sino-American relations in recent years, public opinion in each country has also turned decidedly negative, even outright hostile, toward the other country. Chinese citizens have been increasingly vocal in criticizing their government for not standing up to the United States and for being too soft on Taiwan, and they support an early resolution of Taiwan's status. Although they would prefer a peaceful approach to the use of force, they are overwhelmingly supportive of using force should the island declare independence (Pan et al., 2017; Sinkkonen, 2013). On the other side of the Pacific, there has also been a rise of negative views of China held by both the American elite and public. A survey conducted by the Chicago Council on Global Affairs in 2019 reported that 59 percent of its respondents opposed Washington sending troops to fight China on Taiwan's behalf (Smeltz et al., 2019: 20). One year later in 2020, a rather significant shift occurred. Fifty-four percent of the respondents in a survey conducted by the Center for Strategic and International Studies saw China as the most serious challenger to the United States, outdistancing the number of those who saw Russia in this role (22%) by a large margin. When they were asked to place on a scale of 1 (least) to 10 (most) to indicate their willingness to defend Taiwan if it comes under Chinese threat, the mean response was 7.93 for the opinion elites in this survey and 6.69 for the general public. Thus, there had been a huge change in Americans' views on providing support to Taiwan – even if it meant war with China.

The combination of various considerations discussed above appears to present almost a "perfect storm" that has understandably produced flashing red lights warning a possible impending war over Taiwan. This view is confirmed in recent days by top U.S. military officials, who have issued warnings about the looming danger of a Chinese invasion of Taiwan. These warnings have become increasingly more specific, suggesting that this danger may come to pass sooner than many people expect.

For instance, Admiral John Aquilino, the top officer of the U.S. Indo-Pacific Command, testified to Congress in March 2024, stating that China's military will be ready to invade Taiwan by 2027 (Dress, 2024). His predecessor, Admiral Philip Davidson, issued an even more dire warning in predicting that China will attack Taiwan by 2027 (Tanaka, 2023). In a similar vein, U.S. Air Force General Mike Minihan has predicted that the United States and China will be at war in 2025 (Kube & Gains, 2023). He told his officers to get ready for this conflict by firing "a clip" at a target, and "aim for the head." There might be an element of hyperbole in statements such as this one, but U.S. officials do not typically go on a limp to publicize such warnings.

One just need to recall that both they and their civilian superiors were quite reticent to issue warnings about an impending Japanese attack on the eve of Pearl Harbor, even though they were in possession of a considerable amount of evidence pointing to such a possibility (e.g., Janis, 1982; Wohlstetter, 1962) – and not without good reason for fear of sounding a false alarm, giving away the secret that the United States had successfully decoded Japan's diplomatic cipher MAGIC, and exacerbating Japanese apprehensions that could possibly result in an unwanted, premature confrontation. Although there have been in the past episodes of sensationalism and exaggerated threats in domestic U.S. political debates such as Senator Joseph McCarthy's smear campaign to identify communist sympathizers inside the U.S. government in the 1950s and the so-called missile gap between the United States and the USSR in the 1960s, the recent surge of public statements by U.S. military officers appears unusual.

Significantly, Chinese officials have their reasons also to be concerned, anxious, and even alarmed in view of recent U.S. statements and actions. Threat perception can be a two-way street as encapsulated by the term "mirror image" – and not necessarily with respect to the negative connotation that this term is sometimes associated with, namely, that the fears and anxieties being felt by the relevant officials are somehow baseless or unjustified. It does not require a large leap of imagination to understand that Chinese officials may be sensing that their country is entering a period of acute danger. China is now strong enough to cause serious concern in Washington, but not yet strong enough to effectively deter the United States. The unspoken but obvious premise of those

Americans who are advocating a "get tough" policy on China is that they believe the United States still has a military advantage over China now – but perhaps not for much longer.

Stated plainly, the next decade or two presents a window of vulnerability for China; that is, a zone of danger during which the United States can initiate a preventive war against China. This preventive motivation had characterized Germany's leaders producing World War I (Copeland, 2000; Van Evera, 1984, 1999), and perhaps World War II as well. Berlin was concerned that Germany was poised to experience relative decline, especially in view of the emerging threat from a rising colossus to its east, namely, Russia/the USSR. Instead of seeking to challenge and displace Britain's hegemonic position in the world (which London had already lost to Washington prior to 1914, and certainly by 1938), Germany waged war to remove a perceived threat originating from a rising Russia/the USSR. This interpretation obviously contradicts conventional depiction of the origin of the two world wars as primarily an Anglo-German contest over which one of these two countries should dominate the world (e.g., Organski & Kugler, 1980).

Michael Beckley (2023) has presented an interesting twist that departs from my remarks just now. He argues that the danger to international peace does not actually come from rising powers or declining powers. Rather, peaking powers – those that have experienced high growth rates but have entered a period of economic slowdown – are the ones that tend to be most expansionist in seeking exclusive foreign economic zones, practicing protectionism, and raising armament expenditures. Thus, according to Beckley, the danger facing the United States is not the long-run marathon of economic competition with China. The danger zone is more immediate in that China appears to be headed for, if not having already entered, a period of anemic and perhaps even negative growth which can be a source of both internal and external instability. Whether the United States might be a "peaking or peaked power" was not considered by Beckley.

This is not the time or place for an extended discussion on preventive war, but a few brief remarks may still be appropriate. The administration of George W. Bush had explicitly invoked the logic of preventive war even though it had misnamed it as a "preemptive war" in justifying its invasion of Iraq (on preemptive war, see Reiter, 1995; on preventive war, see Bell & Johnson, 2015; Levy, 1987, 1996, 2008a; Schweller, 1992; Silverstone, 2007; Trachtenberg, 2007). For those who are inclined to reject the idea that a democracy can launch an unprovoked preventive war against another country (e.g., Schweller, 1992), it is both theoretically possible and has actually happened before such as when Israel attacked Iraq's Osirak nuclear reactor and when the Anglo-Franco-Israeli

22   *Indo-Pacific Security*

coalition attacked Egypt in 1956. The United States had come close to launching an attack on North Korea during the Clinton administration, and it had also considered bombing China's nuclear facility at Lop Nor (Burr & Richelson, 2000/2001; Levy, 2008a).

For readers who may think the idea of the United States starting a preventive war against China to be ludicrous and outlandish, consider the report by Bob Woodward and Robert Costa (2021) that in the waning days of the Trump administration, the top U.S. military officer – General Mark Milley, the Joint Chief of Staff – felt that he had to make secret phone calls to his Chinese counterpart, General Li Zuocheng, on October 30, 2020, and again on January 8, 2021, to assuage Chinese concerns that the United States might be considering a preventive war. General Milley was reportedly worried that Donald Trump might become unhinged or, in the words of this report, "go rogue" by starting a nuclear war in the final days of his presidency. He was quoted saying to his Chinese counterpart, "General Li, I want to assure you that the American government is stable and everything is going to be OK. We are not going to attack or conduct any kinetic operations against you . . . . Gen. Li, you and I have known each other now for five years. If we're going to attack, I'm going to call you ahead of time. It's not going to be a surprise" (quoted in Morris, 2021: no page). Thus, even the top U.S. military officer had concerns about his own government starting a nuclear war – or at least concerned enough that Chinese officials might have been seriously concerned about this prospect – to incline him to risk Trump's ire by making these phone calls. When Milley's phone calls were disclosed by the media, Trump reacted predictably, accusing the general of having committed a "treasonous act" that is "so egregious that, in times gone by, the punishment would have been DEATH!" (de Vries, 2023: no page number).

The main point of this discussion is that the U.S. military is not only concerned about China making plans to attack Taiwan but also concerned that the Chinese may also have serious apprehensions and misgivings about U.S. intentions, that they (the Chinese) were seriously worried that the United States might be planning an attack on China – concerned enough for the top U.S. military officer to apparently bypass the usual protocol to reassure his Chinese counterpart. Thus, both sides appear to agree that there is a serious danger of war breaking out. This episode lends some support to my earlier claim that the top leaders of both China and the United States have a good understanding of their counterparts' concerns, motivations, and redlines, although obviously it alone does not suffice as conclusive evidence to clinch my claim.

One more implication from Germany's diplomacy prior to the outbreak of World War I deserves a brief discussion, because it offers a strong parallel to China's current situation. I have argued that World War I happened *not* because

Taiwan and the Danger of a Sino-American War 23

Germany, typically depicted as a cocky and impatient upstart, was itching for a fight to displace Britain as the global hegemon, and Berlin's real target was rather a rising Russia. In my previous research (Chan, 2020), I have argued that Berlin had in fact tried to persuade London to stay on the sideline. That Britain decided eventually to jump into the fray thus indicated a failure of German diplomacy. Similarly, should a war happen between China and the United States, it would not be because Beijing had wanted to seize the mantle of global hegemon from Washington. Beijing's goals are more regional just as for Berlin in 1914. And as with Germany, should the United States decide to intervene militarily in a crisis over Taiwan, it would mean a failure of Chinese diplomacy to persuade Washington to stay out of its civil war. Fighting the United States would be far from Beijing's first preference – it would be its last resort.

Current prevailing discourse in the United States and more generally in the West, such as discussions based on power-transition theory (Organski & Kugler, 1980) and Thucydides' Trap (Allison, 2017), emphasizes the changing balance of power between major states to be the primary reason for systemic war. Power-transition theory in particular argues that these conflicts are started by cocky, revisionist rising states seeking to displace the incumbent hegemon and to overthrow the existing world order. The brief reference to preventive war in my discussion just now disagrees with this proposition. It argues that wars can also be initiated by an established but declining state. Both rationalist theory of war (e.g., Fearon, 1995; Powell, 1999) and prospect theory (e.g., Kahneman et al., 1982; Kahneman & Tversky, 1979, 2000; McDermott, 1998) support this view – even though these theories come from opposing premises about how people make decisions. The discussion in the remainder of this Element suggests that the United States has acted more like a revisionist power, including its policies toward Taiwan (see also Chan, 2020; Chan et al., 2021; Chan & Hu, 2025; Lind, 2017).

There is little doubt that China and the United States agree that should an armed conflict occur between them, it is most likely to occur over their disagreement about Taiwan. This much has been made abundantly clear by the words of these countries' top leaders. On the Chinese side, officials have repeated publicly and privately that the resolution of the Taiwan problem is *the* top priority for them, a core interest of their country. They will not compromise on the fundamental principle of China's sovereignty over Taiwan, and they are determined to complete their mission of national reunification. Deng Xiaoping had told Gerald Ford that Taiwan's status is *the* issue between the United States and China (Zhang, 2024: 34, 131). When Xi Jinping met Joe Biden at the sideline talks on the occasion of the most recent Asia Pacific Economic Cooperation (APEC) summit meeting held in San Francisco in December 2023, he said directly and plainly that Taiwan represents the "biggest" and "most dangerous issue" between the two countries. As with other Chinese leaders, Xi clearly sees the United States as the main stumbling block in China's attempt to achieve national reunification. In Beijing view, had it not been for this U.S. support for Taiwan, or at least Taipei's conviction that Washington "has its back," Taiwan's leaders would have been much more receptive to Beijing's overtures.

Biden said to Xi in their 2023 meeting that the United States has a commitment to defend its "Indo-Pacific allies" (Hou, 2023: no page number). This statement leaves some room for ambiguity because Taiwan is not a formal U.S. ally. Washington had unilaterally abrogated its defense treaty with Taipei when it switched its diplomatic relationship from Taiwan to China. Although the U.S. Congress has passed the Taiwan Defense Act pledging to provide the island with "defensive" weapons, this is a unilateral domestic legislation that is not equivalent to an international treaty – as it can be rescinded unilaterally by the United States at any time.

Biden was more explicit about U.S. intention on other occasions. He responded "yes" when asked whether the United States would intervene on Taiwan's behalf in the event of a Chinese attack on at least four different occasions (August 2021, October 2021, May 2022, and September 2022; *Time Magazine*, 2022; Wingrove, 2022). Officials from his own administration had tried each time to "walk back" his words, claiming that there had not been any change in official U.S. policy on Taiwan. Beijing was naturally incredulous, refusing to believe that these were accidental slips of tongue by the U.S. president rather than deliberate signals to warn China. Such clumsy attempts to "have one's cake and eat it too" do not enhance U.S. credibility in the long term.

In 1972, the United States and China had issued a joint communique, stating, "The United States acknowledges that all Chinese on either side of the Taiwan Strait maintain that there is but one China and that Taiwan is a part of China. The United States Government does not challenge that position. It reaffirms its interest in a peaceful settlement of the Taiwan question by the Chinese themselves" (Taiwan Documents Project, no date). The word "acknowledge" was chosen deliberately to indicate that the United States had taken note of China's position on Taiwan rather than accepting or agreeing with it. The basic thrust of this document, however, is clear. The reference to "Chinese themselves" indicates that people on both sides of the Taiwan Strait are *Chinese* rather than from two separate nations. Indeed, this same document refers to "all *Chinese* on either side of the Taiwan Strait," thus again indicating unambiguously that the United States recognizes the inhabitants on both sides of this strait to be Chinese, and not one side being Chinese and the other side being Taiwanese. Naturally, the U.S. policy has shifted since then, causing Beijing to complain

Taiwan and the Danger of a Sino-American War   25

that the United States has reneged on its agreement with China. In other documents signed with China, the United States. had promised to reduce its arms sales to Taiwan and eventually cease them entirely.

Beijing naturally interprets recent actions and statements by U.S. officials, including Biden's remarks, as a betrayal of Washington's commitments made to it. There was, of course, also the visit by Nancy Pelosi, the then speaker of the U.S. House of Representatives, to Taiwan. She was the third highest ranking U.S. official. Her trip in August 2022 as well as earlier ones by other U.S. officials such as Secretary of Health and Human Services Alex Azar in 2020 broke the long-standing practice of *not* having any serving U.S. official visit the island or having any official contact with the government in Taiwan. This included an informal ban on meeting Taiwan's officials on U.S. government premises, a long-standing practice that has also been abandoned in recent years. Not only has the United States continued to sell weapons to Taiwan but the value of these sales has also increased over the years – contrary to Washington's earlier pledges. Former U.S. Secretary of State in the Trump administration Mike Pompeo has openly called for the United States to recognize Taiwan diplomatically, meaning to grant it the status of a sovereign, independent state (Blanchard, 2022). Finally, there is an ongoing debate in the United States about whether Washington should replace its policy of strategic ambiguity (to be discussed later) with a new policy committing Washington explicitly and publicly to Taiwan's defense (e.g., Georgetown University Initiative for U.S.-China Dialogue on Global Issues, 2020; Gilley, 2010; Glaser et al., 2020; Haass & Sacks, 2020; Zelleke, 2020).

Whether these U.S. actions and statements represent a salami tactic to gradually shift Washington's policy toward increasing support for Taiwan or whether they have been intended as trial balloons to probe Beijing's reaction and test its resolve, one cannot be certain. But from Beijing's perspective, none of the plausible interpretations – including bureaucratic incompetence, verbal slipups, or partisan games in Washington – can be good news for it. It would be a stretch for any Chinese official to believe that the collective significance of these recent developments to mean anything but a shift of U.S. policy to increase Washington's support for Taiwan – not just for this island's continued *de facto* independence but also sending it encouraging signals to declare *de jure* independence.

The very fact that a debate is taking place in Washington to change its existing policy of strategic ambiguity to an outright recognition of Taiwan's statehood and a public pledge of U.S. military support in a possible war cannot but be disconcerting to Beijing and to be seen by it as having the intent or the effect (or both) of emboldening Taiwan's pro-independence politicians. These signs may presage an official (i.e., publicly declared) change of U.S. policy – or at least indicate that the consensus on Washington's policy toward China and Taiwan has broken down. Again, one can perhaps dismiss the significance of individual events occurring in the United States, but collectively there is little doubt that they mean a serious downturn in Sino-American relations. Biden's public statements that the United States would intervene militarily to help Taiwan and his imposition of additional tariffs on Chinese goods (such as electric vehicles and solar panels) provide the latest confirmation of this assessment. As Bob Dylan's song says, you don't need a weatherman to know which way the wind is blowing.

3 Reasons Why Neither China Nor the United States Would Let Go of Taiwan

One often hears the trope that Chinese nationalism and communism are responsible for Beijing's aggressiveness toward Taiwan. Yet a moment's reflection (at least for those who have some casual acquaintance with Chinese history) tells us that the same Chinese nationalists and communists had made major territorial concessions in their various boundary disputes (e.g., Fravel, 2005, 2007/2008, 2008). In particular, they had recognized Mongolia's sovereignty and independence, even though large stretches of this country's territory had been ruled by the Qing Dynasty. Mongolia is about the size of Alaska and the world's eighteenth largest country. Beijing and Ulan Bator established formal diplomatic relationship in 1949. Ironically, the United States did not extend diplomatic recognition to Mongolia until 1987! Indeed, even in the late 1980s, one can still see official maps displayed in Taiwan showing Mongolia to be part of China. Of course, those who ruled Taiwan then might be nationalists – but hardly communists.

Being a nationalist often has a negative connotation in discourse on foreign policy; nationalism is somehow a property of foreigners but seldom a trait that describes oneself. Survey research, however, shows that Americans and Canadians are more nationalist than Chinese, if nationalism means pride in one's own country (Chan, 2024). It is always a good idea to try to put oneself in another's shoes. One may proceed by setting aside the matter of ostensible Chinese nationalism and Beijing's agenda for national reunification by asking: Why can the United States not let go of Cuba? Cuba's geostrategic position to the United States offers the closest parallel to Taiwan's position vis-à-vis China. The United States had plotted the assassination of Fidel Castro, orchestrated and supported an invasion of Cuba at the Bay of Pigs, pushed the world to the brink of a nuclear war over Soviet missiles installed on that island, and has continued its policy of economic embargo against it. China has not done any of these things to Taiwan – at least recently or publicly to my knowledge. What can account for this U.S. conduct? I suspect that not many Americans would subscribe to the explanation that capitalism and nationalism had made the United States so antagonistic to Cuba.

Perhaps the place to look for an explanation of why the United States would not let go of Cuba is to understand this island's importance in domestic U.S. politics. During the Cuban Missile Crisis, some U.S. officials, especially the Secretary of Defense Robert McNamara, were not initially perturbed by news of Soviet missiles in Cuba. A missile is a missile – whether it is fired from a Soviet submarine cruising along the U.S. eastern seaboard or from Cuba. But the political optics compelled the Kennedy administration to act. Some of Kennedy's advisors reportedly said that although the nation (i.e., the United States) might not be threatened by the Soviet missiles in Cuba, the presidency would certainly be in peril if Kennedy was perceived by the American people to be indecisive or irresolute in addressing the presence of Soviet missiles on that island. Not only were the Democratic Party's candidates expected to face setback in the then upcoming Congressional elections but the subject of the president's impeachment had also come up in conversations between the Kennedy brothers (Allison, 1971: 188, 194–5).

Not to put too fine a point on it, in commenting on Britain's decision to go to war to retake the Falklands/Malvinas from Argentina, a cabinet member told a reporter, "To be frank, I don't see how she [Margaret Thatcher] can survive [politically] if she shrinks from a military showdown" (quoted in Lebow, 1985: 117). Chinese leaders are no different; they have to be ever mindful of their domestic political opponents and their legitimacy in the eyes of their people. If U.S. leaders believed that they could not politically afford to "let Cuba go," imagine the political predicament facing any Chinese leader being accused of "letting go of" Taiwan. Stated plainly, my introduction of Cuba in this discussion is intended to ask: How has another great power, namely the United States, acted toward a small wayward neighbor even when the alleged combustible elements of nationalism, irredentism, and communism are excluded as plausible explanatory factors?

There is, however, more than domestic political consideration involved for Chinese – and U.S. – leaders' understanding of the stakes involved in Taiwan's status. This island commands enormous geostrategic importance for China. It is the key to China's front door (Chan & Hu, forthcoming/b), a position comparable to that of Belgium in the lead-up to World War I. Whether France, Germany, or Britain gained control of Belgium, this country could use it as a base to threaten the other two. There were good reasons for these major powers to have pledged to respect Belgium's neutrality in perpetuity, and also for Britain to finally commit itself to fight after German troops invaded it on their way to attack France. Similarly, there is good geostrategic reason why there is an ongoing war in Ukraine, a remark that should of course not be taken to condone Russia's invasion. Ukraine occupies the traditional pathway for invaders to attack Russia, and conversely for Russia, it represents the gateway to Eastern Europe. Geostrategic writers such as Halford MacKinder (1904, 1919, 1943) have averred that whichever country controls Eastern Europe controls the Eurasian Heartland, and whoever controls the Eurasian Heartland controls the World Island and from there the entire world. To a lesser extent, other writers such as Nicholas Spykman (1942, 1944) and, more recently, Zbigniew Brzezinski (1986) also assigned pivotal importance to the world's so-called Heartland. Old-fashioned geopolitical jostling among the great powers has not disappeared even though the forces of globalization have reshaped these contests (Agnew, 2023).

To return our focus to Taiwan, if a foreign power controls this island, it will gain a valuable staging area to attack China; conversely, if China gains control of it, it will be able to use it as a barrier to defend itself and fend off more effectively foreign encroachment. In the hands of an enemy, Taiwan can be used to disrupt and interdict China's north-south traffic and communication. It is also a dagger pointed at China's eastern seaboard, its soft underbelly where the center of its economic, political, and demographic gravity is located. Its geostrategic importance to China is no less than that of Korea which provides a land bridge to China's Northeast, which used to be its center of heavy industries, and over which China had fought the United States when it was much weaker than today. In General Douglas MacArthur's words, Taiwan is an unsinkable aircraft carrier. Taiwan also constricts the access of China's merchant and naval vessels to the open Pacific. Chinese submarines will have to transit through narrow passages on their way to the open Pacific and they can thereby be detected, tracked, and, if need be, intercepted and destroyed before they reach their destination. Given China's weaker capability in waging anti-submarine warfare, the strategic gains conferred by control of Taiwan are even greater for it than for the United States. Brendan Green and Caitlin Talmadge (2022) have discussed in detail Taiwan's enormous military value to China, especially in contributing to the effectiveness of its submarine fleet and enhancing its ocean surveillance capabilities. Their analysis, of course, also suggests the converse – Taiwan's importance to the United States in its effort to deny this island's assets to China. Finally, Taiwan is a valuable outpost to gather signal intelligence and in the earlier years of the Cold War, as a base to send saboteurs and raiders to harass Chinese authorities and attack Chinese infrastructure. *Ceteris paribus*, the closer a conflict site is to a country's home turf, the greater is its stake in this conflict.

Put simply, Washington also cannot "let go" of Taiwan for the same reasons that Beijing is unwilling to "let go," that is, to maintain a geostrategic advantage to bottle up China in the U.S. containment policy. I use the words "to bottle up" deliberately to convey the sense that Taiwan is tantamount to a cork to prevent the content of a bottle from spilling out. In his testimony to the U.S. Senate, Assistant Secretary of Defense Ely Ratner (2001: 1) explained the reasons why the United States would also not "let go" of Taiwan, stating "Taiwan is located at a critical node within the first island chain, anchoring a network of U.S. allies and partners – stretching from the Japanese archipelago down to the Philippines and into the South China Sea – that is critical to the region's security and critical to the defense of vital U.S. interests in the Indo-Pacific." In plain English, Taiwan is the pivot for the U.S. containment policy in East Asia – this containment policy has never been dismantled even after the Cold War's end. And it was implemented long before China's more recent rise. Should Taiwan "fall," it would unsettle the entire *cordon sanitaire* established by the United States in East Asia. As I said, U.S. and Chinese leaders understand each other perfectly, and they agree completely on the geostrategic importance of Taiwan. It is this importance rather than democracy, human rights, and self-determination that concerns Washington.

China faces a fundamentally different geostrategic environment than the United States, which has the good fortune of having only two much weaker countries and fish as its neighbors. In contrast, China shares Germany's predicament of being located in a congested neighborhood and surrounded by powerful neighbors. It ties with Russia in having the largest number of contiguous neighbors. This geographic fact is important because boundary or territorial disputes are the leading cause of military conflicts (Vasquez, 1993, 2009). Yet even without controlling statistically for this variable, the United States has many more militarized disputes, wars, and instances of resort to force than China. Of all the countries, it is odd for the United States to tell others that military force is not the most appropriate way to solve complex international problems. One does not have to condone or agree with Benjamin Netanyahu's government to also see that Washington does not feel the same compunction to refrain from meddling in another country's domestic politics, including that of an ally, as it routinely complains about other countries' interference in its own domestic politics.

Simply put, no U.S. military planner in his or her right mind would want to exchange places with their Chinese counterpart. China, ever since when the People's Republic was established in 1949, has been surrounded by formal and informal U.S. allies on all sides except to its north – and this just recently because there was a time when the USSR and China were bitter enemies and there were rumors that the Kremlin had considered military action against China (it was Moscow that had broached the idea with Washington to strike jointly at China's nuclear facility at Lop Nor). Taiwan has played a crucial part in Washington's strategic plan to contain China.

Taiwan is therefore important to both China and the United States for hard-nosed geostrategic considerations, and not some sentimental reason. One often hears nowadays that Beijing may consider a naval blockade of Taiwan in order to coerce it to accept reunification with China on Beijing's terms. One rarely if ever hears in public discourse in the United States that this role can be reversed – that is, this island can be used as the linchpin to impose a blockade on China. Parenthetically, the fear of becoming the victim of such blockade or resource embargo was the proximate reason for Japan's policies leading up eventually to its fateful decision to attack Pearl Harbor – incidentally, another conflict that leaders had chosen deliberately with their eyes wide open even though they realized that their country (i.e., Japan) was much weaker than their opponent, the United States (Barnhart, 1987; Russett, 1969).

Parenthetically, one also often hears nowadays in the United States that China is challenging the freedom of navigation when in fact compared to the United States, China has a much greater stake in upholding this freedom because it is much more vulnerable to a naval blockade. After all, China has joined the United Nations Law of the Sea (UNCLOS). Even though Washington routinely criticizes Beijing for challenging a "rules-based international order," it has itself refused to join UNCLOS and it has rejected the verdict of the International Court of Justice that it had violated international law for mining Nicaragua's ports. Beijing has likewise refused to accept the jurisdiction of International Arbitration Tribunal to adjudicate the complaint lodged by the Philippines to contest China's assertion of sovereignty in parts of the South China Sea.

As for Japan in the late 1930s and early 1940s, China faces the same prospect of economic strangulation as a result of a possible U.S.-led and -imposed naval blockade. Its reliance on foreign trade and resources is exposed to this vulnerability because its shipping has to pass through several narrow straits. This challenge to China's security has been described as its "Malacca nightmare" in obvious reference to the Malacca Strait. This and other chokepoints enable the U.S. Navy to interdict Chinese commercial shipping. Commenting before more recent improvements in China's naval capabilities (but in 2011 which was not so long ago), Aaron Friedberg (2011: 228) remarked that China would not be able to do anything to overcome such interdiction or blockade by the United States. Naturally, this Chinese maritime vulnerability is not unrelated to Beijing's Belt, Road Initiative to develop an alternate overland route to conduct trade with and ensure the supply of resources from and through Central Asia.

Taiwan and the Danger of a Sino-American War

Cuba does not pose nearly the same level of geostrategic threat to the United States as Taiwan does to China. A glance at its location in the Caribbean indicates that Cuba cannot possibly be used to block or interdict U.S. shipping on both its east and west coast with their unimpeded access to the Atlantic and Pacific Ocean, respectively. This may be also a good place to interject a remark about Ukraine, whose war with Russia was mentioned briefly earlier. No matter how hard the United States tries to frame the discourse on Taiwan's status, it is in one fundamental respect different from the Russo-Ukrainian War (for similarities and differences between Ukraine and Taiwan's situations, see Chan, 2022a; Chan & Hu, forthcoming/b). The overwhelming majority of states in the world recognize Taiwan to be part of China and a matter of China's domestic affair. In contrast, Ukraine is a sovereign, independent state recognized by other states in the world. This basic distinction should be kept in mind. As former U.S. Secretary of State Henry Kissinger has remarked, "for us to go to war with a recognized country . . . over a part of what we would recognize as their country would be preposterous" (quoted by Tyler, 1999: 225).

The ongoing Russo-Ukrainian War is a prime example of war by proxy intended to wear down an adversary's energy and deplete its resources without, however, engaging in a direct fight against it. It is reminiscent of Washington's support of the *mujahadeen* resistance to the USSR's invasion of Afghanistan, and Chinese and Soviet support for Hanoi during the Vietnam War. Ukraine is different from Taiwan, however, because it has land borders with sympathetic neighbors which can provide material support for its fight against Russia. It will be much more difficult for the United States and its allies to provide similar support to Taiwan in case of war because it is an island, and the Chinese will surely try to interdict these countries' effort to supply this aid by sea. At the first sign of an impending war, maritime freight insurance for merchant ships traveling to Taiwan will skyrocket and most, if not all, of this shipping will cease. Civilians will not be able to escape easily from the war zone as in the case for Ukraine, which, as just mentioned, has land borders and rail connections with several sympathetic neighbors. The stock market and the real estate market in Taiwan will collapse. Unlike Ukraine, it is much more questionable whether Taiwan will be able to hold out against a direct Chinese assault for long, not necessarily because the Chinese invading force will be able to easily overcome Taiwan's defense but rather due to mass panic.

Finally, it is difficult to believe that Washington is exclusively, or even primarily, interested in Taiwan for sentimental or idealist reasons. Its support for this island's government was the strongest during those years when it was ruled under martial law by a one-party authoritarian regime under Chiang Kai-shek, one that suppressed all forms of freedom and denied equal rights to the native Taiwanese population. The United States switched its diplomatic relations to China just about the same time when Taiwan was showing incipient signs of democratization. "Contrary to the popular narrative, the West has supported democracy only when that support has been reinforced by material interests, and rarely, if ever, when it has posed a threat to such interests" (Grigoryan, 2020: 158). For example, Washington has treated popular movements in Ukraine and Armenia differently, and the main reason for this difference had to do with whether their government has an anti-Russian orientation.

Claims that the United States supports Taiwan because it is a democracy or because Washington is committed to its people's right of self-determination are not credible. The United States was complicit in the overthrow of democratically elected leaders such as Iran's Mohammad Mosaddegh and Chile's Salvador Allende. Although it has alleged Russian, Chinese, and Iranian interference in U.S. elections, it has been the most flagrant and repeat offender in subverting other countries' elections, as far back as the Central Intelligence Agency's attempt to deny electoral victory to the Italian Communist Party in 1948 (e.g., Levin, 2020). It had supported and continues to support authoritarian regimes that suppress human rights. As for the right of self-determination, it has not extended this right to the Crimeans, the Kashmiris, the Kurds, or the Palestinians, and it had initially opposed the breakaway of Bangladesh from Pakistan. The United States has condemned the secession of Crimea and four oblasts in eastern Donbas from Ukraine, claiming that their plebiscites were illegal because they did not comply with Ukraine's constitution and that their secessions had to be approved by the entire Ukrainian people. It does not, however, apply the same principles to Taiwan. Indeed, it would not be too difficult to determine whether Washington is sincerely committed to the right of self-determination by the people in Taiwan. If this island were to declare independence tomorrow, would the United States support this decision? The entire public rationale given by Washington to justify its policy of strategic ambiguity is supposed to *prevent* Taipei from declaring formal independence in exchange for Washington to deter an armed attack by China – regardless of the preference of the island's inhabitants.

Rote incantations referring to Taiwan as a self-ruling democracy that has never been ruled by Beijing omit important historical details, not the least of which is the fact that the United States had supported it even more strongly when it had an authoritarian government and when Washington had insisted that the government in Taipei was the legitimate government of China – the entire country of China, consisting of both the mainland and the island of Taiwan – and was hence in its view entitled to the China seat in the United Nations long before it became a democracy. This policy held sway of course when the Kuomintang

Taiwan and the Danger of a Sino-American War 33

government did not exercise any control over the Chinese mainland. It is also disingenuous to claim that Taiwan has never been ruled by Beijing, because it elides over the fact that this phenomenon was due to U.S. military intervention and that China's national government controlled by the Kuomintang did rule Taiwan after Japan's surrender in 1945. Washington has reversed its policy completely, now denying that China has any legitimate claim over Taiwan – even though it used to claim that Taiwan under Kuomintang's rule represented China.

On the question of secession, Vladimir Putin has said, "If someone thinks that Kosovo can be granted full independence as a state, then why should the Abkhaz or the South-Ossetian people not also have the right to statehood!" (quoted in Toal, 2017: 154). What goes around sometimes comes around. Just as in regard with Washington's current stance on Taiwan's status, it has treated the *civil* wars in Korea and Vietnam as an *international* conflict with one side crossing an interstate boundary to commit aggression against the other side. This is not the way that U.S. history books talk about Union soldiers crossing the Mason Dixon Line. It is of course not the only country that goes through these rhetorical contortions. Other countries have also been guilty of policy inconsistencies and double standards.

Although Washington was quick to lead NATO (North Atlantic Treaty Organization) to attack Serbia for committing ethnic cleansing, it was slow to condemn Israel's actions in Gaza and looked the other way when genocide was unfolding in Rwanda (Power, 2001). The litany can go on. Although one can overlook isolated episodes, it is difficult to dismiss the more general pattern that has persisted over time. The ensemble of evidence suggests that U.S. support for Taiwan is not due to lofty liberal ideals or any sentimental reason – and Taiwan's people and officials also realize and understand the fact that the island is a pawn in great powers' competition. Significantly, Taiwan people's confidence in the prospect of Washington coming to their defense actually *declined* in the wake of the Russo-Ukrainian War and Biden's public statements that the United States would intervene in the event of a Chinese attack (e.g., Central News Agency, 2022; Liao, 2022; Wang & Cheng, 2024). After all, the United States did *not* send troops to fight for Ukraine.

The United States had undertaken two large military interventions in East Asia, but in both cases, its partners South Korea and South Vietnam could hardly be argued to represent a democracy or a paragon of respect for human rights on whose behalf Washington had fought a long, costly war. *Realpolitik* reasons, especially the containment of Chinese influence (in prior years as a part of an ostensible monolithic international communist bloc), trumped any liberal impulses. To the extent that ideas played a role, they were related to the so-called lesson of Munich and the domino theory.

4 Strategic Ambiguity, Moral Hazard, and Prudent Statecraft

As mentioned earlier, Washington has pursued a policy of strategic ambiguity with respect to Taiwan's status until recently when it has moved closer to committing to this island's defense. Strategic ambiguity is basically supposed to be a policy of dual deterrence (Crawford, 2003). It is supposed to deter Taiwan from declaring independence and Beijing from attacking Taiwan. This policy seeks to do so by refusing to pre-commit the United States to any specific course of action, reserving for it the discretion to decide how to act later when necessary. It in effect puts Washington in the self-appointed role of a referee or judge who is supposed to preside over the two disputants, ensuring that they would not get into a fight and to punish the one that it determines to have committed a transgression. This policy of strategic ambiguity, however, cannot persuade Beijing to overlook that its practical effect is to ensure the preservation of Taiwan's *de facto* independence by thwarting any attempt by Beijing to seize this island by force. As remarked earlier, although until recently Beijing lacked the military capabilities to coerce Taiwan, it has now developed substantial capabilities to do so. As time passes and Beijing acquires more capabilities, why should it put up with a policy intended to perpetuate Taiwan's *de facto* independence indefinitely (supposedly in exchange for it to eschew *de jure* independence)?

As Thomas Schelling (1966: 36) has remarked, "the difference between the national homeland and everything 'abroad' is the difference between threats that are inherently credible, even if unspoken, and threats that have to be made credible." France's president Charles de Gaulle had famously questioned the reliability of U.S. commitment to defend his country, when he insisted that France must have its own independent *force de frappe*. To paraphrase him, would the U.S. government be willing to strike Moscow or St. Petersburg in defense of Paris, if this action would risk the destruction of New York or Chicago in a Soviet retaliation? De Gaulle's obvious skepticism shows the difficulties faced by a defender trying to offer extended deterrence on behalf of a third party (for studies of extended deterrence, see Huth, 1988a, 1988b; for discussions specific to Taiwan, see Chan, 2003, 2005, 2014)?

How can a government seeking to deter an attack on its protégé convince the would-be attacker not to undertake this action? James Fearon (1997) has argued that it can "sink costs" to demonstrate that it means business, such as by committing itself to defend the protégé by signing a defense treaty with it, deploying its own troops on the frontline where they would suffer casualties in a possible enemy attack (thus having these troops serve as a "trip wire"), installing military bases on the protégé's territory, and forming a joint military command with this partner. In all these respects, the United States has made its commitment to the defense of South Korea and Japan much more credible than its intention to fight on Taiwan's behalf. Fearon argues that the heavier the sunk costs, the greater the defender's credibility to fight for its protégé. A sincere defender's willingness to bear these costs distinguishes it from a fake one. That is, a willingness to take on heavy *ex ante* costs distinguishes a serious defender from one that is just pretending.

The other course of action mentioned by Fearon for making the defender's pledge to come to the aid of its protégé credible is for its high-level officials to profess their intention publicly, repeatedly, and loudly – that is, "tying their hands" by deliberately ruling out other policy options and staking their political reputation to their announced intention to defend the protégé. By doing so, they expose themselves to the costs of political fallout that they would have to pay should they renege on their promises. Recent research, however, has shown that the actual political penalty that leaders have suffered for failing to honor their promises or for making empty threats has been rather small (e.g., Snyder and Borghard, 2011; Trachtenberg, 2012). This finding thus questions the effectiveness of tying leaders' hands as a strategy to make their deterrence pronouncements credible. Even if leaders have to pay this cost, it only happens *ex post* – that is, only when insincere leaders are exposed as liars. In other words, these leaders would have gotten away with their lies if their bluff had not been called.

The main point of this discussion is of course that by declining to make an explicit prior commitment to defend a protégé, a policy of strategic ambiguity lacks inherent credibility, and it is thus likely to be dismissed as hot air or empty talk. Fearon explains this matter straightforwardly: How would the target of a deterrence threat expect a sincere defender to act? Would this defender say I will definitely fight you should you cross the redline to attack my protégé, or would it say I *may* fight you? Fearon thus believes that deterrence threat entails a binary choice: to fight or not to fight on behalf of a protégé. Anything short of a definitive commitment is not credible to the target of the deterrence threat. Moreover, this commitment has to be made credible by costly actions. The greater the sunk costs the defender is willing to bear in defense of its protégé, the greater the credibility of its commitment. These costs distinguish a sincere defender from a phony one.

There is, however, a good reason for a policy of strategic ambiguity. It pertains to moral hazard, that is, the possibility that a firm commitment to defend the protégé may incentivize it to provoke war to advance its own interests rather than those of the defender such as the example I mentioned earlier about London's hesitancy to fully commit itself to support France prior to World War I. Just as a protégé lives in constant fear of being abandoned by its more powerful protector, this latter country is concerned about the risk of entrapment by its junior partner. Brett Benson (2012) has studied how the defender sometimes tries to hedge its commitment to its protégé in order to reduce this risk.

Parenthetically, by announcing that the option of sending U.S. troops to fight on Ukraine's behalf was "off the table," the Biden administration's deterrence threat against Russia's invasion was of course compromised from the very start. It had in effect signaled to Moscow that Washington would treat Ukraine differently from any of its NATO partners facing the danger of a possible invasion. Of course, that Taiwan is not a formal ally of the United States also diminishes the credibility of U.S. threat to China that it would intervene on this island's behalf. Again, Beijing's leaders would naturally want to ask how a country that is seriously committed to the defense of Taiwan would act compared to one that is just making empty threats or trying to have its way on the cheap by bluffing. Why the ambiguity in U.S. policy if Washington is truly committed to Taiwan's defense? One plausible answer, although not the only one, is that it wants to reserve for itself the option to decide later not to intervene on behalf of its protégé and to reduce the possible damage to its reputation if it decides to do so.

The Russo-Ukrainian War is informative about a more general pattern of U.S. conduct in situations that may lead Washington to become involved in a direct conflict with Moscow or Beijing. In all past situations involving this risk, Washington had actually acted rather prudently to avoid the danger of having to take on the USSR/Russia or China directly (Chan, forthcoming/b). Thus, for example, it had refrained from intervening when Moscow suppressed the Hungarian uprising in 1956, crushed the Prague Spring in 1968, and fought Georgia in 2008. Washington also took precautions to avoid a combustible situation from escalating in the two episodes of Chinese shelling of the offshore islands Quemoy and Matsu in 1954–5 and 1958, and in the U.S. war in Vietnam lest China decide to intervene in that conflict as it had done in Korea (Whiting, 1962, 1975). Judged by its conduct in these episodes, given its practice heretofore of strategic ambiguity, and for yet other reasons to be introduced in the next section, the probability of the United States intervening militarily in a situation that would put it in a direct fight with China over Taiwan is in my view smaller than current media reports and academic discourse seem to imply.

My remarks here about Washington's prudent policies in past conflict situations suggest that this history should be taken into account in considering my discussion earlier about preventive motivation to wage war. It is relevant and important to recognize that although U.S. leaders had considered launching a surprise attack against Soviet missiles installed in Cuba, China's nuclear test site at Lop Nor, and most recently North Korea's weapons facilities, they decided in the end to pull back from these actions.

It is also important to recognize that Taiwan also has a vote in how things will turn out. It may be unfamiliar for Americans to hear that in the past, U.S. partners and allies have more often restrained Washington from reckless policies than vice versa (Beckley, 2015; Priebe et al., 2021). Taipei is acutely aware that should there be a war, it will be the first, the most direct, and the biggest casualty. Despite the rhetoric of its pro-independence politicians, my sense is that Taipei has also acted quite prudently, except possibly on a few occasions during Chen Shui-bian's presidency. There is a Chinese saying, "listen to the other party's words, watch its deeds" (听其言，观其行). As Fearon has reminded us, the second part of this injunction is more important than the first part. Words have to be backed up by deeds to be credible.

In this respect, there is an obvious puzzle due to the discrepancy between Taiwan's continuing asymmetric dependency on trade with China, on the one hand, and the pro-independence rhetoric of some of its leading politicians, on the other hand. Ever since Albert Hirschman's (1945) influential book, students of political economy have been made aware of the serious political consequences of economic reliance on another country. Why then has Taiwan continued to trade intensely with and invest heavily in China? Don't its politicians and officials know that this economic dependency would create political vulnerability, hurting their cause for eventual independence? Surely, they are not so dense to overlook that their economic dependency on China would make it more costly and difficult for them to pursue political independence for Taiwan. Why would they knowingly trap themselves in this *cul de sac* – and to deepen the (economic) hole they are already in with each passing day?

Brett Bension and Emerson Niou (2007) have written about whether Taiwan's politicians and officials are the "politics first" type or the "economics first" type. If they put politics as their top priority, they would obviously *not* continue to trade with and invest in China. That they have continued policies to allow and even encourage increased commerce between the two sides of the Taiwan Strait suggests that they are really the "economics first" type, and not the "politics first" type. Actions speak louder than words. If these politicians and officials are truly committed to Taiwan's independence, they would not enter into close commercial ties with China, making Taiwan more vulnerable to Beijing's coercion. Given the lopsided asymmetry of economic dependency between Taiwan and China, why would these politicians and officials knowingly imperil their goal of Taiwan's independence and increase its vulnerability to political holdup – unless the island's independence is not their top priority?

States typically do not trade with their prospective enemies because this action increases their risk of becoming the target of economic coercion and because trade can make their opponent stronger. Conversely, trade provides *prima facie* evidence that those countries with extensive commercial relations do not expect future hostilities from their trade partners. Thus, not only does trade make the parties involved in this relationship less inclined to fight (because they will suffer more costs and forfeit more benefits due to the disruption caused by war) but it is also endogenous to their expectations of their future relations (Chan, 2006, 2009; Copeland, 1996; Morrow, 2003; Stein, 2003). In other words, those states that do not expect to fight each other in the future tend to trade more.

This logic suggests that Taiwan's leaders have been reasonably level-headed even though their campaign rhetoric directed at the voters and even though their statements made for Americans' consumption may indicate otherwise. How can Beijing distinguish Taiwan politicians' election rhetoric and pro-U.S. expressions from their true inclinations? By watching their conduct rather than relying on their words which can be just hot air. In this respect, close commercial ties between the two sides of the Taiwan Strait can even be intended as a signal by Taipei – sinking costs in Fearon's terminology – to indicate that it does not intend to "rock the boat" and to reassure Beijing that Taipei does *not* intend to go independent (Chan, 2006, 2009, 2012). Taiwan's economic stake in its close trade and investment relations with China therefore can be interpreted as an act of hostage giving to communicate the seriousness of its intention. Should there be a war across the Taiwan Strait, the costs that will be borne by Taiwan's economy would be so self-evidently huge and ruinous as to give Taipei an enormous incentive to prevent such a war from happening in the first place. This fact makes all the difference in making Taipei's signal inherently believable. For those who know Chinese history, Chinese emperors had often married off their daughters to potentially hostile foreign leaders in order to indicate their amity – and to provide these relatives as hostages to demonstrate their sincerity. The main point of this discussion lends support to my view that leaders involved in the Taiwan controversy actually understand each other rather well and that we should not confuse public rhetoric with actual intention.

5 Power Balance, Effort Mobilization, and the Long Game

Much of the current literature on a possible war over Taiwan focuses on the shifting balance of military capabilities and possible strategies that Beijing may adopt to coerce Taiwan (e.g., Beckley, 2017; Biddle & Oelrich, 2016; Erickson et al., 2017; Gilli & Gilli, 2019; Glosny, 2004; Goldstein & Murray, 2004; Mastro, 2021;

Mearsheimer, 2014; Montgomery, 2014; O'Hanlon, 2000; O'Hanlon et al., 2004; Ross, 2002; Sharp et al., 2018–9). I do not question the general consensus that China has acquired new military capabilities in recent years to tilt the balance between it and Taiwan and between it and the United States more to its advantage – or in some important respects, less to its disadvantage. Nor do I doubt that China still faces formidable challenges in mounting an effective assault on Taiwan whether by amphibious landing or more indirectly by imposing a naval blockade on the island. My reservation has more to do with my view that relative military capabilities and plausible strategies may not tell the whole story or the most important parts of it.

It is well known that smaller or weaker states have sometimes initiated or accepted a fight against a stronger foe, and some of them have managed to prevail – if not as a result of outright victory on the battlefield, then at least by sapping the will and exhausting the patience of their more powerful adversary (e.g., Arreguin-Toft, 2005; Mack, 1975; Merom, 2003; Paul, 1994; Record, 2007). Even though China may be weaker than the United States, Washington has to fight farther away from its home base in a war involving Taiwan. Moreover, China is not Afghanistan, Iraq, or even Vietnam. Washington's own war games and military simulations have reportedly indicated that its intervention will face significant adverse odds. Fareed Zakaria (2020: 68) writes, "The Pentagon has reportedly enacted 18 war games against China over Taiwan, and China has prevailed in every one." This observation leads me to in turn stress four considerations.

First, a country's performance in different policy areas, including its performance on the battlefield, depends to a significant extent on its policy capacity, which includes its government's ability to extract, mobilize, and deploy effectively resources from its society and economy. Research by Jacek Kugler and Marina Arbetman (1997) and Kugler and William Domke (1986) showed this policy capacity to be a critical determinant of the outcomes of different combat theaters during the two world wars and in other conflicts such as the Russo-Japanese War and the contest between North and South Vietnam. The results of their analyses show that actual performance on the battlefield depends on the effective mobilization of available resources rather than the mere possession of these resources. For instance, Japan was the most effective belligerent state in World War II in mobilizing and deploying its resources, enabling it to perform much better than its smaller resource base compared to the other states would have predicted – even though in the end, this greater effectiveness was not enough to offset the disadvantage of its smaller resource base. In contrast, despite its more advanced medical technologies and facilities, the United States suffered more deaths from the Covid-19 pandemic compared to many poorer countries on a per capita basis. Francis Fukuyama (2020) attributes this phenomenon in part to the U.S. government's more limited policy capacity. In addition to this factor, he points to weak leadership and social distrust as causes of the higher U.S. fatality rate relative to other countries.

China's government suffers from many deficiencies and weaknesses, but its policy capacity to penetrate society and mobilize its economy does not appear to be one of them. In contrast, Washington often faces strong social pressure. One of the consequences of this phenomenon is its tendency to wage war without actually raising the necessary funds by imposing an increase on its citizens' taxes, preferring instead to shift the financial burden to future generations by deficit spending. Domestic discord and dysfunctions of various kinds have been known to get in the way of foreign policy, such as when Britain and France under-balanced against an emergent threat from Germany during the 1930s (Schweller, 2006). Moreover, there is the matter of attention deficit. A country such as the United States which has – or sees – its interests engaged in many different parts of the world has a crowded plate that can end up causing indigestion. It is in perpetual danger of being distracted and, even more dangerously, being overstretched as Paul Kennedy (1987) has warned. Finally, it comes simply down to a matter of national priority. Taiwan is at the very top of China's policy agenda. Where does it rank on the list of U.S. objectives?

A government's cohesion, the extent of its elite's consensus, and the degree to which the government and elite enjoy people's trust ad support are all important variables in conducting foreign policy as suggested by my reference just now to Randall Schweller's (2006) book. Available evidence indicates that Americans' trust in their politicians and government is at record low levels, and they are deeply divided on many social, cultural, and political issues. For example, a majority of voters are dissatisfied with *both* initial candidates (Joe Biden and Donald Trump) in the forthcoming 2024 presidential election. Moreover, about one-third of the electorate believe that the current incumbent U.S. president came to office due to electoral irregularities, and Biden was thus not elected legitimately.

Robert Keohane and Joseph Nye have made a general point in line with my reference above to crowded policy agenda, national discord, and attention deficit. They argue that Australia and Canada's cohesion and attention in comparison to that of the United States enabled Ottawa and Canberra to attain more favorable outcomes in their respective disputes with Washington than one would have expected from the asymmetry in these countries' relative power.

Taiwan and the Danger of a Sino-American War 41

> Governmental cohesion is important in determining (dispute) outcomes, and, in general, the United States was less cohesive than Canada and Australia. In part this lack of cohesion is a function of sheer size and of presidential as contrasted with parliamentary government, but it is also a function of asymmetry of attention. The U.S. government does not focus on Canada and Australia the way that Canada, or even Australia, focuses on the United States. Greater cohesion and concentration help to redress the disadvantage in size (Keohane and Nye 1977: 207–8).

Second, and related to my earlier remark, a country's relative stake in a dispute and its resolve to stand its ground also matter. As far as Taiwan is concerned, there is an asymmetry in terms of resolve and commitment to their respective cause on the part of China and the United States. Dedication to one's cause and a willingness to endure hardship are intangibles that are hard to measure, but these factors have surely played an important role in the Vietnam War, for example. Jean-Pierre Cabestan (2024: 91) quoted an anonymous Chinese general questioning Washington's resolve: "you [the United States] care more about Los Angeles than Taiwan!" This general obviously believes that the conflict between China and the United States is fundamentally lopsided in terms of each country's willingness to bear the necessary costs commensurate with their respective stake in this dispute. The logic of my discussion also suggests that China does not have to necessarily prevail militarily over the United States in order to succeed. It just needs to impose more costs than the U.S. government and American people would be willing to bear; that is, if their political or psychological threshold for tolerating pain in its various forms is significantly lower than China's. Therefore, I argue that the dispute between China and the United States over Taiwan is not just a matter of their relative military capabilities. It is also a contest of will.

Nothing can persuade Beijing that Washington cares more about Taiwan than Beijing cares about it. Much evidence shows that when body bags begin to come home, the patience of the American people will be severely tested. Taiwan's leaders are also not so dense and forgetful to overlook that they had already been "abandoned" at least once before when Washington switched its diplomatic recognition from Taipei to Beijing and had abruptly, unilaterally, and cavalierly abrogated its security treaty with Taipei. They do not need to be reminded of what had happened to U.S. allies in Saigon and Kabul. Like the Kelpers in Falklands/Malvinas, Britain is far away but Argentina is close by. Americans can go home one day, but Taiwan will be stuck with its much larger neighbor – just as for Ukraine vis-à-vis Russia. People in Taiwan and China are fully aware that Taiwan is important to Washington because it is important to China – that is, Taiwan's importance to the United States is derivative of Washington's relations with Beijing. It is not intrinsically important despite Washington's rhetoric about defending democracy and human rights. James Fearon (1995) has taught them and us to distinguish credible commitment from hot air. Taiwan serves primarily an instrumental purpose for Washington. There is a joke circulating in some quarters to the effect that Washington is quite prepared to fight the Russians – until the last Ukrainian standing. In the wake of the Russo-Ukrainian war, public opinion polls in Taiwan showed a *drop* in its people's confidence that the United States would come to its aid (Wang & Cheng, 2024).

Third and as just alluded to above, diplomatic and military contests entail a long game. Which side has more stamina and patience? Singapore's former prime minister Lee Kuan Yew was asked at a public forum about his opinion on whether the United States would intervene militarily in a crisis involving Taiwan. His answer was quick and to the point. He said "no" (https://www .youtube.com/watch?v=q_gr3dtBaic). His reason? The United States may be able to prevail the first time. But how about the next time, and the time after that? And so on? China is more dedicated to its cause, and it will be more able to play the long game while the United States is more likely to become impatient, distracted, or disillusioned. Lee's point is of course that if U.S. leaders take the long term into consideration, they would not get their country into this morass in the first place.

War propensity depends of course on the calculus of both prospective belligerents. It takes two to tangle. As discussed earlier, these states' decisions on whether to fight have to do with their relative stake in a conflict and their relative resolve in addition to their relative capabilities. Even more relevant, would the stakes involved justify the risks and costs they will each have to bear? Based on its past conduct, Washington is likely to conclude in the negative with respect to Taiwan – barring a major change in the cast of those responsible for U.S. policymaking. Stated simply, what exactly are the U.S. vital interests in the dispute over Taiwan's status to warrant Washington to take on the risks and costs of fighting Beijing with all its attendant consequences, including the specter of nuclear war?

One important consideration, however, tends to weaken my prognosis of the improbability of a Sino-American war. According to prospect theory, it is easier to deter an actor from making a potential gain than compelling it to accept an actual loss (Levy, 2008b: 542). Thus, there is an asymmetry in psychological motivation which tends to favor the defender of the status quo (in this case, Washington and Taipei). This said, if Beckley (2023) is right in arguing that Beijing's growth has peaked, prospect theory suggests that its leaders may see themselves entering a period of relative loss (compared to its prior rate of growth or to other countries' growth rates). Prospect theory predicts that actors in the domain of actual or expected loss will pursue riskier policy. This expectation would of course also apply to the United States as a country in relative decline attempting to reverse or arrest this loss.

Finally, these remarks sound a warning about not to stake a country's reputation on a problematic policy. The tragedy of Vietnam – and of Iraq and Afghanistan – lies in Washington's eagerness to "sell" its war to a skeptical American public. In undertaking this public relations campaign, U.S. officials exaggerated the extent to which vital U.S. interests were at stake. They trapped themselves in their own rhetoric (Thomson, 1973), making a subsequent policy reversal more difficult to undertake for political and psychological reasons, and consequently causing more serious damage to U.S. reputation when the reversal was eventually undertaken because, after all, officials had said publicly and repeatedly that vital U.S. interests were at stake. This practice reduces the government's credibility the next time it tries to convince the American people of the necessity of fighting another war, which forces the government to "market" its policy even harder to convince a more skeptical public. Vietnam, Iraq, and Afghanistan became important for U.S. reputation because Washington had said and made them important, declaring that they were a test of its will. It set up its own test question – and failed it.

After the bombing of the U.S. marine's barracks in Beirut in 1983, the so-called Weinberger Doctrine was introduced. It stipulated that the United States should not undertake military intervention abroad unless a number of conditions are met. On the top of this list of conditions is that truly vital U.S. interests must be at stake. In 1948–9, Washington had practically made up its mind that it would wash its hands of the Chiang Kai-shek regime and to disengage itself from the Chinese Civil War. This decision was reversed due to an accidental development. The outbreak of the Korean War led to Harry Truman's order to the Seventh Fleet to "neutralize" the Taiwan Strait. The aftereffects of this decision are still being felt today.

6 Conclusion: The Danger of Overreach and Self-Entrapment

I have argued that Sino-American differences on Taiwan's status reflect a real clash of geostrategic interests more than some ideational differences, sentimental reasons, or emotional impulses. Although ideas such as democracy, human rights, nationalism, self-determination, national and ethnic identity, and grievances about or memories of perceived past injustices are certainly also involved in the dispute between these two countries, I tend to give more analytic weight to considerations about Taiwan's geostrategic location to hinder and contain China's projection of its military and political power and to subject its coastal economy, communication, and overseas trade to the risk of disruption and blockade. Given these considerations, if Taiwan is allied with the United States, it provides a forward base for hostile forces to directly threaten the Chinese mainland. Conversely, if China controls the island, it would have broken through the first island chain established by the United States to impair and deny China's access to the open Pacific. Besides geostrategic reasons, any Chinese leader seen to be weak on reclaiming Taiwan will jeopardize his or her political career given the domestic political setting – and in this sense, nationalism does matter, albeit more in the domestic context which of course influences Beijing's foreign policies in this indirect way. Taiwan's parallel with Cuba reminds us that we can learn something important from past U.S. conduct toward this small Caribbean nation even when neither national reunification nor communist ideology is presumably relevant to Washington's policy calculations.

More controversially, I argue that the policy of strategic ambiguity practiced by Washington heretofore has not been very credible in persuading Beijing about the seriousness of U.S. deterrence threat to protect Taiwan, nor has Washington's own conduct in past conflicts suggested that it will throw caution to the wind to risk a direct clash with the USSR/Russia or China. In other words, Washington has acted in the past quite prudently in these situations, having seemed to have learned its lesson of underestimating Beijing's resolve and capabilities in its encounter with China in Korea. In one of the most thorough and thoughtful studies on the Vietnam War, Yuen Foong Khong (1992) has used documentary analysis and process tracing to explain the seeming puzzle that the Lyndon Johnson administration had consistently chosen military options that the top U.S. officials realized to be less effective in coercing Hanoi but were in their view more prudent in avoiding the danger of Chinese intervention – even though they were told by their intelligence agencies that in the absence of a U.S. invasion of North Vietnam, this contingency was unlikely. Concern about possible Chinese intervention was one of the constant themes in U.S. policy deliberations. In Khong's (1992: 146) words, "the need to avoid drawing China into the [Vietnam] war, seems to have been most influential."

The U.S. experience in Iraq and Afghanistan would also have a sobering influence on its policy in a possible crisis involving Taiwan. Similarly, Beijing has thus far acted rather cautiously in situations that may escalate into a direct confrontation with Washington, such as when it deescalated the Offshore Island Crises in 1954–5 and again in 1958. That China has not attacked Taiwan suggests in my mind that in addition to the extent of Sino-American capability disparity heretofore, the potential devastation caused by war – in ways more than just physical destruction – would be in Beijing's eyes so great as to present a pyrrhic victory even if it prevails militarily.

Taiwan and the Danger of a Sino-American War

As just mentioned, Beijing had acted cautiously in prior crises in the Taiwan Strait, having pulled back on these occasions to avoid escalation potentially risking a war with Washington. That Beijing had decided to pull back on these occasions without having successfully altered the status quo could be interpreted as a setback for it. One strong implication follows from this observation. Why would it try again in view of this prior experience? Rationalist explanation of war would suggest that if Beijing tries again, Chinese leaders must have become more resolved to have their way and/or more optimistic of having their way this next time. In other words, Washington would be facing a more determined foe and/or one that believes its chances of success are greater this next time (Chan, 2003, 2005, 2014; rationalist theorists would refer to "private information" to explain this greater resolve or optimism).

Important differences exist between past situations (such as in the 1950s and even the 1995–6 crisis when Beijing was greatly upset with Taiwan president Lee Teng-hui's visit to the United States and his inflammatory speech in its view at his alma mater Cornell University) and now, and between situations involving the USSR/Russia and China. These differences incline me to surmise that the prospect of U.S. military intervention on behalf of Taiwan is smaller than many recent discussions such as "Ukraine today, Taiwan tomorrow" would lead one to expect. For one thing, China has more economic clout than Russia. Unlike Russia's relations with the European countries, China is the most important trade partner for most Asian countries. Any attempt to sanction Beijing will impose a heavy cost on the sanctioning countries as well.

Besides, most recent estimates suggest that Russia's economy has done reasonably well in view of Western countries' economic sanctions (https://www.russiamatters.org/blog/has-war-ukraine-destroyed-russias-economy). The reason for Moscow's better-than-expected economic performance has been due substantially to the refusal of many developing economies, such as China, Brazil, and India, to join the West's policy of economic coercion. Of course, there are also recent signs – especially from the United States – that enthusiasm to support Ukraine has waned significantly. The U.S. Congress authorized funding to assist Ukraine only after a long delay and protracted negotiation due to partisan differences over other issues.

Naturally, China has also increased its military capabilities significantly in recent decades compared to past conflicts when it was much weaker, including when the United States was fighting in Vietnam but exercised considerable restraint (such as refraining from invading North Vietnam and bombing the Red River dikes). Thus, while I would certainly not deny that a clash over Taiwan is the most likely cause for a Sino-American confrontation, my intuition is that this danger is not as great as some current discussions appear to suggest.

Lastly, I infer substantial restraint on Washington's part in the most recent situation roiling the Middle East. In the aftermath of the conflict between Hamas and Israel, there were firefights involving other groups such as the Hezbollah, the Houthis, and other combatants affiliated with Iran. The Houthis had shelled maritime traffic transiting the Red Sea. While striking back against Houthi targets and even after Tehran had fired hundreds of missiles at Israel in an apparent retaliation against Tel Aviv's bombing of Iran's consulate in Damascus killing several of its generals, Washington appeared to have gone out of its way to reassure Iran that it had no intention or interest in enlarging the war against it. This development also contributed to my proposition that the United States would avoid a direct confrontation with China over Taiwan.

Although the possibility of misperception and misinterpretation obviously cannot be ruled out, my relatively sanguine view also reflects my sense that the top leaders of China, the United States, and Taiwan understand their counterparts' concerns, motivations, and redlines better than sometimes suggested in popular and scholarly literature. My greater worry is about political demagogues hijacking the policy processes on any one and even all three sides, thereby creating a spiral of recriminations and acrimonies that legitimate the other side's political extremists, ultranationalists, and militarists. The danger is that each side's hardliners would furnish fuel for their respective foreign counterparts to sustain and even elevate tension. In other words, I tend to see the danger of escalation coming more likely from domestic rather than foreign sources. Each country's hardliners are the best allies of hardliners in other countries. They create and thrive on an echo chamber feeding off reciprocal antipathy.

Taiwan's people and their leaders are quite cognizant of the fact that should there be war, they would be its greatest victims. Put plainly, they are not suicidal. They would rather live with the status quo than rock the boat. At the same time, as I have stated earlier, Chinese leaders appear still confident about their country's future. I agree with Thomas Christensen's (2001) observation that China can pose problems for the United States without catching up. I would even go further to argue that a declining China – facing a serious economic downturn or domestic political chaos – would be more troublesome for the United States than one that is still optimistic about its future status in the world. There is a substantial literature on the so-called diversionary theory war, suggesting that leaders who are in trouble at home would try to distract their people's attention by escalating foreign tension and manipulating international crises to enhance their domestic popularity (e.g., Chiozza & Goemans, 2003; DeRouen, 2000; Haynes, 2017; Meernik & Waterman, 1996; Morgan, 1999; Richards et al., 1993; Smith, 1996; Sobek, 2007). The Argentine generals' initiation of the Falklands/Malvinas War is a prime exhibit of this tendency.

This is also the conclusion of Robert Powell's (1999) analysis based on the logic of rationalist theory of war. As argued earlier, German leaders' fear of their country's relative decline was the source of their preventive motivation leading to the two world wars. In contrast, a rising China should be a satisfied China and it should be less inclined to overthrow the international order that has facilitated its ascent. This view of course contradicts power-transition theory's claim. I have never been able to understand this theory's argument that an established but declining country should continue to support the existing international order rather than seeking to revise its rules in order to arrest and reverse its decline. The other side of the argument – that a rising state is somehow necessarily motivated, if not hardwired, to overthrow the existing international order – also seems to me to be quite problematic.

Although, as already indicated, I see the top leaders in Beijing, Washington, and Taipei to have a good understanding of one another, I do not dismiss the sense of concern, anxiety, and even alarm that can develop from perceptions of ongoing power shifts in Taipei and Washington, and conversely, a sense of overconfidence and arrogance that may affect Beijing's policymakers. The danger posed by structural transformation of the international system – as highlighted in power-transition theory and Thucydides' Trap – in arousing these emotions can have quite real consequences. Leaders can be influenced by ongoing or expected power shifts to initiate preventive war, as the Germans did in the two world wars – conflicts that they had started deliberately with their eyes wide open.

Again, this remark should not be misconstrued to suggest that only a currently stronger state but one that is experiencing or poised to experience relative decline in the future will be so motivated. After all, currently weaker states that expect further decline in the future have also been known to start war, such as Pakistan in August 1965, Egypt in October 1973, and Japan in December 1941 (Chan, 2024b). My surmise – and in these matters, it is hard to be dogmatic – is that in the next decade or so, the danger of a war between China and the United States may become greater, thus offsetting the other reasons I mentioned earlier that contribute to prudent policies for all three parties being entangled in the dispute over Taiwan's status. This is the dangerous period during which China would be still weaker and not capable of deterring the United States effectively but at the same time strong enough to arouse U.S. anxiety and cause its animosity. In subsequent years, I expect the power balance between these two countries to become more equalized, and the threat of war to abate compared to the future that lies immediately ahead. These remarks therefore point to the operation of cross currents, some having a stabilizing influence and others a destabilizing influence. On the whole,

I see the former forces to be stronger than the latter forces, but their interactions can also change over time as just suggested. We are dealing with a dynamic situation that can evolve quickly.

I expect that China will continue to catch up to the United States, thereby creating a situation of more balanced power between these countries, which in turn will contribute to stabilizing their relationship. Although the latter proposition reflects the traditional tenet of realism, it obviously challenges the more recent popular view suggesting that power parity between China and the United States, or the approach to power parity, is fraught with danger. Some people may very well disagree with my contention. Lest I be misunderstood, I do not expect China to be able to sustain in the coming years its torrid rate of economic growth in the decades after 1979. In fact, I expect China's nearly double-digit rate of past growth to fall substantially. China does face some economic headwinds, such as its contracting labor force. As the German saying goes, trees do not grow to the sky.

The direction of ongoing trends and the speed of change are important considerations that will define the parameters for policymaking. As alluded to in the preceding paragraph, time is not neutral. The question then becomes which side is likely to benefit more from the passage of time. Of course, no one has a crystal ball, but my hunch is that China will continue to close the capability gap separating it from the United States. At the same time, the capability asymmetry between Taiwan and China will continue to grow – which in turn means that Taipei will become increasingly reliant on U.S. support to sustain its *de facto* independence and that its bargaining position vis-à-vis Beijing will become weaker in the future. It is a tricky balancing act for Taipei. It has to figure out whether and, if so, when to strike a deal with Beijing. It is the party that is truly caught in the horns of a dilemma, facing the Scylla of putting all its eggs in the same basket by counting exclusively on U.S. support and the Charybdis of being left alone facing China and succumbing to its pressure to reach a deal on Beijing's terms.

Taiwan's predicament can be in part traced to its earlier decision to discontinue its program to develop nuclear weapons because of U.S. pressure. Because of this decision, it is now less able to deter China credibly and more dependent on the United States to protect it. Its current predicament may be a "learning moment" for other countries just as in the case of Ukraine, which had agreed to give up nuclear weapons left on its soil after the USSR collapsed. Kyiv gave up these weapons in exchange for security guarantees from London, Moscow, and Washington in the so-called Budapest memorandum, and it is currently suffering from the consequences of this decision. Naturally, realism does not typically expect countries with the wherewithal to protect their own national security to

Taiwan and the Danger of a Sino-American War 49

subcontract it to another country – such as Japan and Germany's reliance on the United States and Ukraine's misplaced faith in British, American and Russian commitments.

Ironically, the looming threat to Taiwan stems in part from other episodes involving the use of force by the United States. Although the Bush administration had used the threat of Saddam Hussein's development or possession of weapons of mass destruction to justify its invasion of Iraq, many people in Moscow, Beijing, and other capitals now suspect that it had invaded Iraq precisely because Washington did *not* think Iraq in fact had these weapons or else it would have hesitated to attack that country. In contrast, after Mohammad Qaddafi invited international inspection to prove that he did not have weapons of mass destruction in order to avoid Saddam Hussein's fate, the West proceeded to attack Libya, which eventually led to his gruesome death. Ironically, the one country in the "axis of evil" declared by the Bush administration that did have nuclear weapons – namely, North Korea – had not been attacked by the United States. And another country that could quickly develop these weapons, namely, Iran, has also thus far avoided being attacked by Washington. When asked about what lesson he drew from the NATO attack on Serbia in 1999, an anonymous Indian general reportedly said, "Don't fight the U.S. unless you have nuclear weapons" (quoted in Chan, 2008: 150). Thus, reputation does matter – although not in the usual way in which many commentators and pundits in the United States and some of its former officials have argued in advocating stronger support for Taiwan lest Washington's reputation is tarnished by a failure to support Taipei. In other words, Washington's past actions have had an effect that conduces nuclear proliferation rather than limiting it.

If the United States "walks away" from Taiwan, its reputation to support its allies and partners will *not* necessarily suffer in my view, although it could encourage other states to develop their own indigenous capability to deploy nuclear weapons. An overwhelming majority of states in the world see Taiwan as a part of China, and the resolution of its status is a matter of Chinese domestic affairs – a legacy of its civil war. They thus perceive this case to be qualitatively different from Ukraine (Chan & Hu, 2025, forthcoming/b). Recent U.S. legislative turmoil causing a delay in providing aid to the latter country is far more damaging to its reputation. Officials in other countries, as well as those in Taiwan, remember that the United States had already "abandoned" Taiwan at least once before when Washington de-recognized it to switch its diplomatic tie to China.

Reputation (for resolve and reliability) is what states make of it. In the past, serious damage to U.S. reputation has been due to its own exaggerated rhetoric to justify its involvement in Korea, Vietnam, and Afghanistan. This damage reflects self-entrapment, and it can also be due to foreigners' perception of Washington engaging in deliberate misrepresentation as in its propagation of its ostensible reasons for attacking Iraq and Libya ("weapons of mass destruction," "links with Al Qaeda," "humanitarian intervention"). It pays to be honest in life and diplomacy (Sartori, 2005).

It has often been argued that a country should redouble its effort in continuing a policy that has not been working and that it should try harder in order to honor the sacrifices made by those who have died. It is not clear to me how the logic of this argument works, and it sounds like an argument for throwing good money after a bad investment. A country's stake in a conflict should determine in the first place whether it should get into this conflict – rather than reversing the logic by arguing that having gotten into a conflict, the country now has a stake in it to protect its reputation and honor its dead.

Prospect theory has an explanation for this view, calling it "gambling for recovery." Those in the domain of loss are psychologically motivated to take more risks to reverse their fortune (e.g., Kahneman et al., 1982; Kahneman & Tversky, 1979, 2000; McDermott, 1998). They are also resistant to abandoning a failed policy because it means coming to terms with a loss. As in other areas of policymaking, policy stasis usually holds sway for a variety of reasons, including institutional rigidity, cognitive limitations ("muddling through"), a general conservative tendency in policymaking ("incrementalism"), and just people's limited capacity to process information ("bounded rationality") (e.g., Lindblom, 1959; Simon, 1957, 1977; Wildavsky, 1964, 1975). Sequential attention to problems often compounds these tendencies, especially when one administration gets a country into a foreign mess, leaving another administration to fix it.

The default is always the continuation of an existing policy – meaning that the necessary change often comes too late because, in addition to those factors just mentioned, time, attention, and political capital and courage are always in short supply. The result, as explained earlier, is that often the damage caused by a wrong policy and domestic dysfunctions to a country's reputation is all that much greater. Pericles had warned his fellow Athenians "not to extend your empire at the same time as you are fighting the war [in Sicily] and not to add self-imposed dangers, for I am more afraid of our own mistakes than the strategy of our opponents" (quoted in Kagan, 1969: 192). This discussion suggests that self-inflicted injuries, such as those caused by rhetorical trap, institutional rigidity, and personal ego, can do more damage to a country than the plots of a clever enemy.

There is another source of self-inflicted injury. Susan Shirk (2023) wrote recently about serious mistakes made by Beijing both domestically and in its relations with other countries. In the latter regard, Chinese foreign policies in

Taiwan and the Danger of a Sino-American War

her view have alienated and alarmed its neighbors, causing what has been described as "self-encirclement" in the context of the consequences brought about by Wilhelmine Germany's brusque and aggressive conduct of *Weltpolitik* (e.g., Murray, 2010; Snyder, 1993; Wolf, 2014). Such behavior is another example of self-defeating policy. Still another example of such unforced error comes to mind. Paul Kennedy (1987: 515) has warned about the danger of imperial overstretch caused by a mismatch in a country's objectives and the resources available to it to pursue these objectives, warning that

> the United States now runs the risk, so familiar to historians of the rise and fall of previous Great Powers, of what might be called "imperial overstretch": that is to say, decision-makers in Washington must face the awkward and enduring fact that the sum total of the United States' global interests and obligations is nowadays far larger than the country's power to defend them all simultaneously.

Pericles had warned his fellow Athenians, "Nor can you now give [the empire] over for already your government is in the nature of a tyranny, which is both unjust for you to take up and unsafe to lay down" (quoted in Platias and Trigkas, 2021: 229).

The United States tends to see its interests engaged all over the world. In contrast, China tends to have a more regional focus, attending more closely to matters pertaining to its immediate neighborhood. Taiwan is clearly at the very top of its policy priorities. Compared to China, the United States has a more crowded agenda and is more likely to be distracted by many more issues and torn by competing interests. When seen in terms of the ratio of available resources – which of course include time, policy attention, and political capital – to perceived interests, Washington is more likely to become strained and subject to the risk of overreach. A traditional Chinese strategy to cope with a stronger opponent is to send it on a wild-goose chase – sapping its energy, depleting its resources, diverting its attention, and, finally, undermining its will.

China controls the initiative of timing with respect to Taiwan. It can wait for an opportune time when the United States is distracted by another crisis or overburdened by engagement in other theaters to take action about Taiwan. It is in a better position to play a waiting game than the hyperactive United States. Kennedy's warning about imperial overstretch would become more germane and urgent if conflicts in different parts of the world become "nested" or intertwined – such as if there are concurrent crises going on in Europe such as the Russo-Ukrainian War, in the Middle East such as a conflict between Israel and Syria plus Iran, in South Asia involving Pakistan and India, and finally in East Asia involving Taiwan and/or Korea. Recent events suggest such a scenario involving multiple, simultaneous conflicts is not out of the realm of possibilities. Should it come to pass, the threat to overstretching resources, including policy attention, becomes more real and pressing.

Daniel Treisman (2004) has written about Spain's foreign policy during the reigns of Philip III and Philip IV. These monarchs were determined to crush all perceived opposition in the belief that Madrid had to demonstrate its resolve in order to deter future challenges. This policy, however, turned out to be self-defeating. By getting Spain into multiple wars, sometimes concurrently, it exhausted the country militarily, financially, and psychologically – with the counterproductive effect of causing more challenges to these monarchs, both internally and externally, due to the country's exhaustion. It set Spain on a path of inexorable decline from which it was never able to recover. In contrast to Spain's policy of "taking on all comers," Britain practiced a policy of rational and selective appeasement in the years prior to World War I. London accommodated the United States, settled account with Russia, conciliated with France, and even joined Japan in an alliance – all in order to conserve its limited resources to concentrate on the nearby threat emerging from Germany. London's policy made all the difference in how World War I turned out for it.

Before closing, I wish to return to an earlier argument, suggesting that U.S. reputation would not suffer to the extent that proponents of a policy of "resist China, aid Taiwan" contend. Attribution theory tells us that when an unfriendly actor behaves in a "nice" way, people tend to interpret this behavior to mean *not* that it has had a change of heart – or a transformation of its disposition or character – but are instead likely to interpret it to suggest an adverse change in its circumstances (e.g., Mercer, 1996, 2007). For example, when Joseph Stalin unexpectedly withdrew Soviet troops from Austria and decreased the USSR's defense spending, John Foster Dulles, the then U.S. Secretary of State, saw these developments as evidence not of the Soviet leader having changed his stripes and thus becoming nicer. Rather, he saw them as evidence that Moscow was getting weaker, inclining him *not* to reciprocate Stalin's gestures but rather to increase pressure on the Kremlin (Holsti, 1962). Similarly, when the United States withdrew from Vietnam and Afghanistan, Beijing did not see these decisions to indicate a change in Washington's general disposition to be less interventionist henceforth or its intention to refrain from supporting its clients elsewhere such as Taiwan. Attribution theory argues that it is more likely to interpret Washington's behavior as a sign of its changing circumstances, such as greater policy constraints due to rising domestic opposition and resource limitation. Parenthetically, Washington saw Moscow's concessions to the West before and after the Cold War's end to also reflect its weaker capability rather than nicer intention. U.S. leaders pushed harder in

Taiwan and the Danger of a Sino-American War 53

promoting color revolution and regime change in Russia's near abroad. Their reaction to Moscow's objection to NATO expansion was dismissive: "Who cares what they think? They're a third-rate power" (Borger 2016: no page number).

Finally, my proposition about contestants' asymmetric resolve and stake in determining the outcome of conflicts may be controversial. By my reasoning, the United States is likely to decide that the game is not worth the candle. Rhetoric by some of its politicians and officials is likely to end up being empty talk. My relative optimism about a war *not* happening over Taiwan's status reflects my hunch that in the end, Washington will not come through for Taipei. My reasoning is based on the asymmetry in Chinese and U.S. motivations – and not so much on their relative capabilities although, as I have also indicated, these capabilities are trending in a direction more favorable to China (or less unfavorable to it), increasing its *relative* capabilities even while the United States maintains its *absolute* advantage in the immediate future. As conflicts in Korea, Vietnam, and, most recently, Afghanistan attest, a country's relative capacity *and* willingness to mobilize resources, including popular support for and dedication to a political cause, are critical in determining whether peace or war will prevail across the Taiwan Strait and should there be war, how it will turn out. On this important point, I can do no better than Lee Kuan Yew, whose compelling logic on the unlikely prospect of U.S. military intervention on behalf of Taiwan I have introduced earlier. Lee's conclusion obviously takes a long-term view. Of course, both he and I can be wrong. There is nothing to prevent people from being stupid, selfish or myopic.

References

Agnew, J. (2023). *Hidden Geopolitics: Governance in a Globalized World*. Lanham, MD: Rowman & Littlefield.

Allison, G. T. (1971). *Essence of Decision: Explaining the Cuban Missile Crisis*. New York: HarperCollins.

Allison, G. T. (2017). *Destined for War: Can America and China Escape Thucydides's Trap?* Boston, MA: Houghton Mifflin Harcourt.

Arreguin-Toft, I. (2005). *How the Weak Win Wars: A Theory of Asymmetric Conflict*. Cambridge: Cambridge University Press.

Barbieri, K. (2002). *The Liberal Illusion: Does Trade Promote Peace?* Ann Arbor, MI: University of Michigan Press.

Barnett, M. & Duvall, R. (2005). Power in international politics. *International Organization*, 59(1), 471–506.

Barnhart, M. A. (1987). *Japan Prepares for Total War: The Search for Economic Security, 1919–1945*. Ithaca, NY: Cornell University Press.

Baumgartner, F. R. & Jones, B. D. ([1993] 2009). *Agendas and Instability in American Politics*. 2nd ed. Chicago, IL: University of Chicago Press.

Beckley, M. (2015). The myth of entangling alliances. *International Security*, 39(4), 7–48.

Beckley, M. (2017). The emergent balance in East Asia: How China's neighbors can check Chinese naval expansion. *International Security*, 42(2), 78–119.

Beckley, M. (2023). The perils of peaking powers: Economic slowdowns and implications for China's next decade. *International Security*, 48(1), 7–46.

Bell, S. R. & Johnson, J. C. (2015). Shifting power, commitment problems, and preventive war. *International Studies Quarterly*, 59(1), 124–32.

Benson, B. V. (2012). *Constructing International Security: Alliances, Deterrence, and Moral Hazard*. Cambridge: Cambridge University Press.

Benson, B. V. & Niou, E. M. S. (2005). Public opinion, foreign policy, and the security balance in the Taiwan Strait. *Security Studies*, 14(2), 274–89.

Benson, B. V. & Niou, E. M. S. (2007). Economic interdependence and peace: A game-theoretic analysis. *Journal of East Asian Studies*, 7(1), 35–59.

Biddle, S. & Oelrich, I. (2016). Future warfare in the Western Pacific: Chinese antiaccess/area denial, U.S. airsea battle, and command of the commons in East Asia. *International Security*, 41(1), 7–48.

Blanchard, B. (2022). U.S. should recognize Taiwan; former top diplomat Pompeo says. *Reuters*, March 4. www.reuters.com/world/asia-pacific/us-should-recognise-taiwan-former-top-diplomat-pompeo-says-2022-03-04/.

References

Borger, J. (2016). Russian hostility "partly caused by West," claims former US defence head. *The Guardian*, March 9. www.theguardian.com/world/2016/mar/09/russian-hostility-to-west-partly-caused-by-west.

Bourne, K. (1967). *Britain and the Balance of Power in North America, 1815–1908*. Berkeley, CA: University of California Press.

Brzezinski, Z. (1986). *Game Plan: A Geostrategic Framework for the Conduct of the U.S.-Soviet Contest*. Boston, MA: Atlantic Monthly Press.

Bueno de Mesquita, B. & Smith A. (2012). *The Dictator's Handbook: Why Bad Behavior Is Almost Always Good Politics*. New York: PublicAffairs.

Bueno de Mesquita, B., Smith, A., Siverson, R. M., & Morrow, J. D. (2003). *The Logic of Political Survival*. Cambridge, MA: The MIT Press

Burr, W. & Richelson, J. (2000/2001). Whether to "strangle the baby in the cradle:" The United States and the Chinese nuclear program, 1960–64. *International Security*, 25(3), 54–99.

Bush, R. C. (2005). *Untying the Knot: Making Peace in the Taiwan Strait*. Washington, DC: Brookings Institution Press.

Bush, R. C. (2013). *Uncharted Strait: The Future China-Taiwan Relations*. Washington, DC: Brookings Institution Press.

Buzan, B. & Cox, M. (2013). China and the US: Comparable cases of "peaceful rise"? *Chinese Journal of International Politics*, 6(2), 109–32.

Cabestan, J. P. (2024). *Facing China: The Prospect for War and Peace*. Lanham, MD: Rowman & Littlefield.

Campbell, K. M. & Rapp-Hooper, M. (2020). China is done biding its time: The end of Beijing's foreign policy restraint? *Foreign Affairs*, July 15. www.foreignaffairs.com/articles/china/2020-07-15/china-done-biding-its-time.

Campbell, K. M. & Ratner, E. (2018). The China reckoning: How Beijing defied American expectations. *Foreign Affairs*, 97(2), 60–70.

Campbell, K. M. & Sullivan, J. (2020). Competition without catastrophe: How America can both challenge and coexist with China. *Foreign Affairs*, September/October. www.foreignaffairs.com/articles/china/competition-with-china-without-catastrophe?utm_source=academic&utm_medium=email&utm_campaign=CFRAcademicBulletin29Jan2021&utm_term=AcademicBulletin.

Center for Strategic and International Studies (2020). Mapping the future of U.S. China policy: Views of U.S. thought leaders, the U.S. public, and U.S. allies and partners. https://chinasurvey.csis.org/analysis/.

Central News Agency (2022). Public less confident in U.S. coming to Taiwan's defense: Survey. April 30. https://focustaiwan.tw/politics/202204300009.

Chan, S. (2003). Extended deterrence in the Taiwan Strait: Learning from rationalist explanations in international relations. *World Affairs*, 166(2), 109–25.

Chan, S. (2005). Prognosticating about extended deterrence in the Taiwan Strait: Implications from strategic selection. *World Affairs*, 168(1), 13–25.

Chan, S. (2006). The politics of economic exchange: Carrots and sticks in Taiwan, China and U.S. relations. *Issues & Studies*, 42(2), 1–22.

Chan, S. (2008). *China, the U.S., and the Power-Transition Theory: A Critique*. London: Routledge.

Chan, S. (2009). The political economy of détente: Taiwan's economic integration with China. *Maryland Series in Contemporary Asian Studies*, 1, 68–87.

Chan, S. (2012). Money talks: International credit/debt as credible commitment. *Journal of East Asian Affairs*, 26(1), 77–103.

Chan, S. (2014). Extended deterrence in the Taiwan Strait: Discerning resolve and commitment. *American Journal of Chinese Studies*, 21(2), 83–93.

Chan, S. (2020). *Thucydides's Trap? Historical Interpretation, Logic of Inquiry, and the Future of Sino-American Relations*. Ann Arbor, MI: University of Michigan Press.

Chan, S. (2021). In the eyes of storm: Taiwan, China, and the U.S. in challenging times. In C.M. Clark, K. Ho, and A.C. Tan, eds., *Taiwan's Political Economy*. New York: Nova Science Publishers, pp. 61–78.

Chan, S. (2022a). Precedent, path dependency, and reasoning by analogy: The strategic implications of the Ukraine war on Sino-American relations and relations across the Taiwan Strait. *Asian Survey*, 62(5–6), 945–68.

Chan, S. (2022b). 陳思德 (侯秀琴譯), 美國、台灣和華府的戰略模糊政策. *The Storm Media* (風傳媒), December 16. www.storm.mg/article/4659315?mode=whole.

Chan, S. (2023a). *Rumbles of Thunder: Power Shifts and the Danger of Sino-American War*. New York: Columbia University Press.

Chan, S. (2023b). Bewildered and befuddled: The West's convoluted narrative on China's rise. *Asian Survey*, 63(5), 691–715.

Chan, S. (2024). *Culture, Economic Growth, and Interstate Power Shift: Implications for Competition between China and the United States*. Cambridge: Cambridge University Press.

Chan, S. (Forthcoming/a). *Fuses, Chains, and Backlashes: China, the United States, and the Dynamics of Conflict Contagion and Escalation*. Oxford: Oxford University Press.

Chan, S. (Forthcoming/b). *Punctuated Equilibrium and Sion-American Relations*. Cambridge: Cambridge University Press.

Chan, S. (Forthcoming/c). Power shift, problem shift, and policy shift: Reacting to China's rise. In P. Rhamey and S. D. Bakish, eds., *The Sources of Great Power Competition*. New York: Routledge.

References

Chan, S. & Hu, W. (2025). Taiwan as a flash point: Possible lessons from the war in Ukraine. In W. Thompson and T. J. Volgy, eds., *Reconsidering the East Asian Peace: Confluences, Regional Characteristics and Societal Transformations*. New York: Routledge, pp. 155–80.

Chan, S. & Hu, W. (Forthcoming/a). Rising states and the liberal world order: The case of China. *International Affairs*.

Chan, S. & Hu W. (Forthcoming/b). *Geography and International Conflict: Ukraine, Taiwan, Indo- Pacific, and Sino-American Relations*. New York: Routledge.

Chan, S., Feng, H., He, K., & Hu, W. (2021). *Contesting Revisionism: China, the United States, and the Transformation of International Order*. Oxford: Oxford University Press.

Chiozza, G. & Goemans, H. E. (2003). Peace through insecurity: Tenure and international conflict. *Journal of Conflict Resolution*, 47(4), 443–67.

Christensen, T. J. (2001). Posing problems without catching up: China's rise and challenges to U.S. security policy. *International Security*, 25(4), 5–40.

Cohen, M. D., March, J. G., & Olson, J. P. (1972). A garbage can theory of organizational choice. *Administrative Science Quarterly*, 17(1), 1–25.

Copeland, D. C. (1996). Economic interdependence and war: A theory of trade expectations. *International Security*, 20(4), 5–41.

Copeland, D. C. (2000). *The Origins of Major War*. Ithaca, NY: Cornell University Press.

Crawford, T. W. (2003). *Pivotal Deterrence: Third-Party Statecraft and the Pursuit of Peace*. Ithaca, NY: Cornell University Press.

Daalder, I. H. & Lindsay, J. M. (2005). *America Unbound: The Bush Revolution in Foreign Policy*. New York: Wiley.

DeRouen, K., Jr. (2000). Presidents and the diversionary use of force: A research note. *International Studies Quarterly*, 44(2), 317–28.

De Vries, K. (2023). Milley says Trump disrespected US military with execution comment. Cable News Network (CNN), September 28. www.cnn.com/2023/09/28/politics/milley-donald-trump-execution-comment/index.html.

Diehl, P. F., ed. (1998). *The Dynamics of Enduring Rivalries*. Urbana, IL: University of Illinois Press.

Diehl, P. F. & Goertz, G. (2000). *War and Peace in International Rivalry*. Ann Arbor, MI: University of Michigan Press.

Dress, B. (2024). China will be ready for potential Taiwan invasion by 2027: US admiral warns. *The Hill*, March 21. https://thehill.com/policy/defense/4547637-china-potential-taiwan-invasion-2027-us-admiral-warns/.

References

Erickson, A. S., Montgomery, E. B., Neuman, C., Biddle, S., & Oelrich I. (2017). Correspondence: How good are China's antiaccess/area-denial capabilities? *International Security*, 41(4), 202–13.

Farrel, H. & Newman A. L. (2019). Weaponized interdependence: How global economic networks shape state coercion. *International Security*, 44(1), 42–79.

Fearon, J. D. (1994). Signaling versus the balance of power and interests: An empirical test of a crisis bargaining model. *Journal of Conflict Resolution*, 38(2), 236–69.

Fearon, J. D. (1995). Rationalist explanations for war. *International Organization*, 49(3), 379–414.

Fearon, J. D. (1997). Signaling foreign policy interests: Tying hands versus sinking costs. *Journal of Conflict Resolution*, 41(1), 68–90.

Fravel, M. T. (2005). Regime insecurity and international cooperation: Explaining China's compromises in territorial disputes. *International Security*, 30(2), 46–83.

Fravel, M. T. (2007/2008). Power shifts and escalation: Explaining China's use of force in territorial disputes. *International Security*, 32(3), 44–83.

Fravel, M. T. (2008). *Strong Border, Secure Nation: Cooperation and Order in China's Territorial Disputes*. Princeton, NJ: Princeton University Press.

Friedberg, A.L. (2011). *A Contest for Supremacy: China, America, and the Struggle for Mastery in Asia*. New York: Norton.

Friedman, G. & LeBard, M. (1991). *The Coming War with Japan*. New York: St. Martin's.

Fukuyama, F. (2020). The pandemic and political order: It takes a state. *Foreign Affairs*, July/August. www.foreignaffairs.com/articles/world/2020-06-09/pandemic-and-political-order.

Gartzke, E., Li, Q., & Boehmer C. (2001). Investing in the peace: Economic interdependence and international conflict. *International Organization*, 55(2), 391–438.

Georgetown University Initiative for U.S.-China Dialogue on Global Issues. (2020). America's Taiwan policy: Debating strategic ambiguity and the future of Asian security. October 2. https://uschinadialogue.georgetown.edu/events/america-s-tai wan-policy-debating-strategic-ambiguity-and-the-future-of-asian-security.

Gilley, B. (2010). Not so dire straits: How the Finlandization of Taiwan benefits U.S. security. *Foreign Affairs*, 89(1), 44–56, 58–60.

Gilli, A. & Gilli, M. (2019). Why China has not caught up yet: Military-technological superiority and the limits of imitation, reverse engineering, and cyber espionage. *International Security*, 43(3), 141–89.

Glaser, B. S., Mazarr, M. J., Glennon, M. J., Haass, R., & Sacks, D. (2020). Dire straits: Should American support for Taiwan be ambiguous? *Foreign Affairs*,

References

September 24. www.foreignaffairs.com/articles/united-states/2020-09-24/dire-straits.

Glosny, M. A. (2004). Strangulation from the sea? A PRC submarine blockade of Taiwan. *International Security*, 28(4), 125–60.

Goddard, S. E. (2006). Uncommon ground: Indivisible territory and the politics of legitimacy. *International Organization*, 60(1), 35–68.

Goldstein, L. & Murray W. (2004). Undersea dragons: China's maturing submarine force. *International Security*, 28(4), 161–96.

Gramsci, A. (1971). *Selections from the Prison Notebooks of Antonio Gramsci.* New York: International Publishers.

Green, B. R. & Talmadge, C. (2022). Then what? Assessing the military implications of Chinese control of Taiwan. *International Security*, 47(1), 7–45.

Grigoryan, A. (2020). Selective Wilsonianism: Material interests and the West's support for democracy. *International Security*, 44(4), 158–200.

Haass, R. & Sacks, D. (2020). American support for Taiwan must be unambiguous. *Foreign Affairs*, September 20. www.foreignaffairs.com/articles/united-states/american-support-taiwan-must-be-unambiguous.

Haynes, K. (2017). Diversionary conflict: Demonizing enemies or demonstrating competence? *Conflict Management and Peace Science*, 34(4), 337–58.

Hirschman, A. O. (1945). *National Power and the Structure of Foreign Trade.* Berkeley, CA: University of California Press.

Holsti, O. (1962). The belief system and national images: A case study. *Journal of Conflict Resolution*, 6(3), 244–52.

Hou, P. (2023). China won't invade Taiwan – for now. *The Diplomat*, December 8. https://thediplomat.com/2023/12/china-wont-invade-taiwan-for-now/.

Hsieh, J. F. S. & Niou, E. M. S. (2005). Measuring Taiwan public opinion on Taiwanese independence. *China Quarterly*, 181(1), 158–68.

Huth, P. K. (1988a). *Extended Deterrence and the Prevention of War.* New Haven, CT: Yale University Press.

Huth, P. K. (1988b). Extended deterrence and the outbreak of war. *American Political Science Review*, 82(2), 423–44.

Ike, N. (1967). *Japan's Decision for War: Records of the 1941 Policy Conferences.* Stanford, CA: Stanford University Press.

Janis, I. L. (1982). *Groupthink: Psychological Studies of Policy Decisions and Fiascoes.* Boston, MA: Houghton Mifflin.

Jervis, R. (1978). Cooperation under the security dilemma. *World Politics*, 30(2), 167–214.

Johnston, A. I. (2011). Stability and instability in Sino-US relations: A response to Yan Xuetong's superficial friendship theory. *Chinese Journal of International Politics*, 4(1), 5–29.

References

Kagan, D. (1969). *The Outbreak of the Peloponnesian War*. Ithaca, NY: Cornell University Press.

Kagan, R. (2005). The Illusion of "Managing" China. *The Washington Post*. May 15. https://www.washingtonpost.com/wpdyn/content/article/2005/05/13/AR2005051301405.html.

Kahneman, D. & Tversky, A. (1979). Prospect theory: An analysis of decision under risk. *Econometrica*, 47(2), 263–92.

Kahneman, D. & Tversky A., eds. (2000). *Choices, Values, and Frames*. Cambridge: Cambridge University Press.

Kahneman, D., Slovic, P., & Tversky, A., eds. (1982). *Judgment under Uncertainty: Heuristics and Biases*. Cambridge: Cambridge University Press.

Kang, D. C. (2023). There is no East Asian balancing against China. Manuscript.

Kastner, S. L. (2022). *War and Peace in the Taiwan Strait*. New York: Columbia University Press.

Kaufman, C. (2004). Threat inflation and the failure of the marketplace of ideas: The selling of the Iraq war. *International Security*, 29(1), 5–48.

Kennedy, P. (1987). *The Rise and Fall of Great Powers*. New York: Vintage Books.

Keohane, R. O. & Nye, J. S. (1977). *Power and Interdependence: World Politics in Transition*. Boston, MA: Little, Brown.

Khong, Y. F. (1992). *Analogies at War: Korea, Munich, Dien Bien Phu, and the Vietnam Decisions of 1965*. Princeton, NJ: Princeton University Press.

Kim, C. J. (2019). Military alliances as a stabilising force: U.S. relations with South Korea and Taiwan, 1950s–1960s. *Journal of Strategic* Studies, 44(7), 1041–62.

Kube, C. & Gains, M. (2023). Air force general predicts war with China in 2025, tells officers to prep by firing "a clip" at a target, and "aim for the head." *NBC News*, January 27. www.nbcnews.com/politics/national-security/us-air-force-general-predicts-war-china-2025-memo-rcna67967.

Kugler, J. & Arbetman, M. (1997). Relative policy capacity: Political extraction and political reach. In M. Arbetman and J. Kugler, eds., *Political Capacity and Economic Behavior*. Boulder, CO: Westview, pp. 11–45.

Kugler, J. & Domke, W. (1986). Comparing the strengths of nations. *Comparative Political Studies*, 19(1), 39–69.

Kupchan, C. A. & Trubowitz, P. L. (2007). Dead center: The demise of liberal internationalism in the United States. *International Security*, 32(2), 7–44.

Kupchan, C. A. & Trubowitz, P. L. (2010). The illusion of liberal internationalism's revival. *International Security*, 35(1), 95–109.

Kupchan, C. A. & Trubowitz, P. L. (2021a). A China strategy to reunite America's allies. *Project Syndicate*, January 4. www.project-syndicate.org/commentary/biden-china-strategy-to-reunite-us-allies-by-charles-a-kupchan-and-peter-trubowitz-1-2021-01?barrier=accesspaylog.

References

Kupchan, C. A. & Trubowitz, P. L. (2021b). The home front: Why an internationalist foreign policy needs a stronger domestic foundation. *Foreign Affairs*, May/June. www.foreignaffairs.com/articles/united-states/2021-04-20/foreign-policy-home-front.

Larson, D. W. & Shevchenko, A. (2010). Status seekers: Chinese and Russian responses to U.S. primacy. *International Security*, 34(4), 63–95.

Larson, D. W. & Shevchenko, A. (2019). *Quest for Status: Chinese and Russian Foreign Policy*. New Haven, CT: Yale University Press.

Layne, C. (1994). Kant or cant: The myth of the democratic peace. *International Security*, 19(2), 5–49.

Lebow, R. N. (1984). Window of opportunity: Do states jump through them? *International Security*, 9(1), 147–86.

Lebow, R. N. (1985). Miscalculation in the South Atlantic: The Origins of the Falklands war. In R. Jervis, R. N. Lebow, and J. G. Stein, eds., *Psychology and Deterrence*. Baltimore, MD: Johns Hopkins University Press, pp. 85–124.

Lebow, R. N. (2010). *Why Nations Fight: Past and Future Motivations for War*. Cambridge: Cambridge University Press.

Levin, D. H. (2020). *Meddling in the Ballot Box: The Causes and Effects of Partisan Electoral Interventions*. Oxford: Oxford University Press.

Levy, J. S. (1987). Declining power and the preventive motivation for war. *World Politics*, 60(1), 82–17.

Levy, J. S. (1996). Loss aversion, framing and bargaining: The implications of prospect theory for international conflict. *International Political Science Review*, 17(2), 177–93.

Levy, J. S. (2008a). Preventive war and democratic politics. *International Studies Quarterly*, 52(1), 1–24.

Levy, J. S. (2008b). Deterrence and coercive diplomacy: The contributions of Alexander George. *Political Psychology*, 29(4), 537–52.

Liao, G. (2022). Taiwanese pessimistic about prospect of US sending troops to help defend nation: pollster. *Taiwan Times*, May 20. www.taiwannews.com.tw/news/4481985.

Lieber, K. A. (2007). The new history of World War I and what it means for international relations theory. *International Security*, 32(2), 155–91.

Lin, S. S. (2016). *Taiwan's China Dilemma: Contested Identities and Multiple Interests in Taiwan's Cross- Strait Economic Policy*. Stanford, CA: Stanford University Press.

Lind, J. (2017). Asia's other revisionist power: Why U.S. grand strategy unnerves China. *Foreign Affairs*, 96(2), 74–82.

Lindblom, C. (1959). The science of muddling through. *Public Administration Review*, 19(2), 79–88.

References

Liu, F. C. S. (2016). Taiwanese voters political identification profile, 2013-2014: Becoming one China or creating a new country? *Asian Survey*, 56(5), 931–57.

Lukes, S. (1975). *Power: A Radical View*. Houndmills: MacMillan.

Mack, A. (1975). Why big nations lose small wars: The politics of asymmetric conflict. *World Politics*, 27(2), 175–200.

Mackinder, H. J. (1904). The geographical pivot of history. *The Geographical Journal*, 23(4), 421–37.

Mackinder, H. J. (1919). *Democratic Ideals and Reality: A Study in the Politics of Reconstruction*. London: Constable.

Mackinder, H. J. (1943). The round world and the winning of the peace. *Foreign Affairs*, 21(4), 595–605.

Mansfield, E. D. & Pollins, B. M, eds. (2003). *Economic Interdependence and International Conflict: Perspectives on an Enduring Debate*. Ann Arbor, MI: University of Michigan Press.

Mastro, O. S. (2021). The Taiwan temptation: Why Beijing might resort to force. *Foreign Affairs*, 100(4), 58–67.

Mazarr, M. J. (2007). The Iraq war and agenda setting. *Foreign Policy Analysis*, 3(1), 1–23.

Mazarr, M. J. (2020). Dire straits: should American support for Taiwan be ambiguous? A guarantee won't solve the problem. *Foreign Affairs*, September 24. www.foreignaffairs.com/articles/united-states/2020-09-24/dire-straits.

McDermott, R. (1998). *Risk-Taking in International Relations: Prospect Theory in American Foreign Policy*. Ann Arbor, MI: University of Michigan Press.

Mearsheimer, J. L. (2014). Taiwan's dire straits. *The National Interest*, 130 (March-April), 29–39.

Mearsheimer, J. J. & Walt, S. M. (2003). An unnecessary war. *Foreign Policy*, 134 (January/February), 50–59.

Meernik, J. & Waterman, P. (1996). The myth of the diversionary use of force by American president. *Political Research Quarterly*, 49(3), 573–90.

Mercer, J. (1996). *Reputation and International Politics*. Ithaca, NY: Cornell University Press.

Mercer, J. (2007). Reputation and rational deterrence theory. *Security Studies*, 7(1), 100–11.

Merom, G. (2003). *How Democracies Lose Small Wars: State, Society, and the Failure of France in Algeria, Israel in Lebanon, and the United States in Vietnam*. Cambridge: Cambridge University Press.

Montgomery, E. B. (2014). Contested primacy in the Western Pacific: China's rise and the future of U.S. power projection. *International Security*, 38(4), 115–49.

Morgan, C. (1999). Domestic support and diversionary external conflict in Great Britain, 1950–1992. *Journal of Politics*, 61(3), 799–814.

References

Morris, K. (2021). Milley secretly called Chinese officials out of fear Trump would "attack" in final days: Book claims. *Fox News*, September 14. www .foxnews.com/politics/milley-secretly-called-chinese-officials-out-of-fear-trump-would-attack-in-final-days-book-claims.

Morrow, J. D. (1993). Arms versus allies: Tradeoffs in the search for security. *International Organization*, 47(2), 207–33.

Morrow, J. D. (2003). Assessing the role of trade as a source of costly signals. In E. D. Mansfield and B. Pollins, eds., *Economic Interdependence and International Conflict*. Ann Arbor, MI: University of Michigan Press, pp. 89–95.

Murata, K. (2007). U.S.-Japan alliance as flexible institution. In G. J. Ikenberry and T. Inoguchi, eds., *The Uses of Institutions: The U.S., Japan, and Governance in East Asia*. New York: Palgrave Macmillan, pp. 131–50.

Murray, M. (2010). Identity, insecurity, and great power politics: The tragedy of German naval ambition before First World War. *Security Studies*, 19(4), 656–88.

Murray, M. (2019). *The Struggle for Recognition in International Relations: Status, Revisionism, and Rising Powers*. New York: Oxford University Press.

O'Hanlon, M. E. (2000). Why China cannot conquer Taiwan. *International Security*, 25(2), 51–86.

O'Hanlon, M. E., Goldstein, E. L. & Murray, W. (2004). Correspondence: Damn the torpedoes: Debating possible U.S. navy losses in a Taiwan scenario. *International Security*. 29(2), 202–6.

Olson, M., Jr. (1965). *The Logic of Collective Action*. Cambridge, MA: Harvard University Press.

Olson, M., Jr. & Zeckhauser, R. (1966). An economic theory of alliances. *Review of Economics and Statistics*, 48(3), 266–79.

Oren, I. (2003). *Our Enemies and US: America's Rivalries and the Making of Political Science*. Ithaca, NY: Cornell University Press.

Organski, A. F. K. & Kugler, J. (1980). *The War Ledger*. Chicago, IL: University of Chicago Press.

Pan, H. H., Wu, W. C., & Chang, Y. T. (2017). How Chinese citizens perceive cross-Strait relations: Survey results from ten major cities in China. *Journal of Contemporary China*, 26(106), 616–31.

Paul, T. V. (1994). *Asymmetric Conflicts: War Initiation by Weaker Powers*. Cambridge: Cambridge University Press.

Platias, A. & Trigkas, V. (2021). Unravelling the Thucydides' Trap: Inadvertent escalation or war of choice? *Chinese Journal of International Politics*, 14(2), 187–217.

Powell, R. (1999). *In the Shadow of Power: States and Strategies in International Politics*. Princeton, NJ: Princeton University Press.

Power, S. (2001). Bystander to genocide. *The Atlantic*, September. www.thea tlantic.com/magazine/archive/2001/09/bystanders-to-genocide/304571/.

Prestowitz, C. V., Jr. (1990). *Trading Places: How We Are Giving Our Future to Japan and How to Reclaim It*. New York: Basic Books.

Priebe, M., Rooney, B., McCulloch, C., & Burdette, Z. (2021). *Do Alliances and Partnerships Entangle the United States in Conflict?* Santa Monica, CA: RAND.

Putnam, R. D. (1988). Diplomacy and domestic politics: The logic of two-level games. *International Organization*, 42(3), 427–60.

Ratner, E. (2021). Statement by Dr. Ely Ratner, assistant secretary of defense for Indo-Pacific security affairs office of the secretary of defense before the 117th congress committee on foreign relations, *United States Senate*, December 8. www.foreign.senate.gov/imo/media/doc/120821_Ratner_Testimony1.pdf.

Record, J. (2007). *Beating Goliath: Why Insurgencies Win*. Washington, DC: Potomac Books.

Reiter, D. (1995). Exploding the powder keg myth: Preemptive wars almost never happen. *International Security*, 20(2), 5–34.

Renshon, J. (2016). Status deficits and war. *International Organization*, 70(3), 513–50.

Renshon, J. (2017). *Fighting for Status: Hierarchy and Conflict in World Politics*. Princeton, NJ: Princeton University Press.

Richards, D., Morgan, T. C., Wilson, R. K., Schwebach, V., & Young, G. D. (1993). Good times, bad times, and the diversionary use of force: A tale of some not-so-free agents. *Journal of Conflict Resolution*, 37(3), 504–35.

Richardson, L. F. (1960). *Arms and Insecurity*. Pittsburgh, PA: Boxwood Press.

Rigger, S. (2011). *Why Taiwan Matters: Small Island, Global Powerhouse*. Lanham, MD: Rowman & Littlefield.

Ross, R. S. (2002). Navigating the Taiwan Strait: Deterrence, escalation dominance, and US-China Relations. *International Security*, 27(2), 48–85.

Rousseau, D. L. (2006). *Identifying Threats and Threatening Identities: The Social Construction of Realism and Liberalism*. Stanford, CA: Stanford University Press.

Russett, B. M. (1969). Refining deterrence theory: The Japanese attack on Pearl Harbor. In D. G. Pruitt and R. C. Snyder, eds., *Theory and Research on the Causes of War*. Englewood Cliffs, NJ: Prentice Hall, pp. 127–35.

Russett, B. M. & Oneal, J. R. (2001). *Triangulating Peace: Democracy, Interdependence and International Organizations*. New York: Norton.

Sartori, A. E. (2005). *Deterrence by Diplomacy*. Princeton, NJ: Princeton University Press.

Schake, K. (2017). *Safe Passage: The Transition from British to American Hegemony*. Cambridge, MA: Harvard University Press.

References 65

Schelling, T. C. (1966). *Arms and Influence*. New Haven, CT: Yale University Press.

Schroeder, P. (1976). Alliances, 1815–1945: Weapons of power and tools of management. In K. Knorr, ed., *Historical Dimensions of National Security Problems*. Lawrence, KS: University Press of Kansas, pp. 227–62.

Schweller, R. L. (1992). Democratic structure and preventive war: Are democracies more pacific? *World Politics*, 44(2), 235–69.

Schweller, R. L. (2006). *Unanswered Threats: Political Constraints on the Balance of Power*. Princeton, NJ: Princeton University Press.

Sharp, T., Meyers, J. S., & Beckley, M. (2018/2019). Correspondence: Will East Asia balance against Beijing? *International Security*, 43(3), 94–7.

Shirk, S. L. (2023). *Overreach: How China Derailed Its Peaceful Rise*. Oxford: Oxford University Press.

Silverstone, S. A. (2007). *Preventive War and American Democracy*. London: Routledge.

Simon, H. A. (1957). *Models of Man*. New York: Wiley.

Simon, H. A. (1977). The logic of heuristic decision-making. In R. S. Cohen and M. W. Wartofsky, eds., *Models of Discovery*. Boston, MA: D. Reidel, pp. 154–75.

Sinkkonen, E. (2013). Nationalism, patriotism, and foreign policy attitudes among Chinese university students. *China Quarterly*, 216, 1045–63.

Smith, A. (1996). Diversionary foreign policy in democratic systems. *International Studies Quarterly*, 40(1), 133–53.

Smeltz, D., Daalder I., Friedhoff K., Kafura C. & Helm, B. (2019). *Rejecting Retreat: Americans Support US Engagement in Global Affairs*. Chicago, IL: Chicago Council on Global Affairs. https://www.jstor.org/stable/pdf/resrep21408.6.pdf?refreqid=excelsior%3A2fd3e4bb415aa23a893aa608a4885563

Snyder, G. H. (1997). *Alliance Politics*. Ithaca, NY: Cornell University Press.

Snyder, J. (1993). *Myth of Empire: Domestic Politics and International Ambition*. Ithaca, NY: Cornell University Press

Snyder, J. & Borghard, E. D. (2011). The cost of empty threats: A penny, not a pound. *American Political Science Review*, 105(3), 437–56.

Sobek, D. (2007). Rallying around the podesta: Testing diversionary theory across time. *Journal of Peace Research*, 44(1), 29–45.

Solingen, E. (2007). Pax Asiatica versus bella Levantina: The foundations of war and peace in East Asia and the Middle East. *American Political Science Review*, 101(4), 757–80.

Spykman, N. J. (1942). *America's Strategy in World Politics: The United States and the Balance of Power*. New York: Harcourt, Brace.

Spykman, N. J. (1944). *The Geography of the Peace*. New York: Harcourt, Brace.

Stein, A. A. (2003). Trade and conflict: Uncertainty, strategic signaling, and interstate disputes. In E. D. Mansfield and B. M. Pollins, eds., *Economic Interdependence and International Conflict*. Ann Arbor, MI: University of Michigan Press, pp. 111–26.

Taiwan Documents Project. (No date). Shanghai communiqué: 28 February 1972. www.taiwandocuments.org/communique01.htm.

Tanaka, M. (2023). Ex-U.S. Indo-Pacific commander sticks to 2027 window on Taiwan attack. *Kyoto News*, January 23. https://english.kyodonews.net/news/2023/01/018a26a02962-ex-us-indo-pacific-commander-sticks-to-2027-window-on-taiwan-attack.html.

Thompson, W. R. (1995). Principal rivalries. *Journal of Conflict Resolution*, 39(2), 195–223.

Thomson, J. C. (1973). How could Vietnam happen? An autopsy. In M. H. Halperin and A. Kanter, eds., *Readings in American Foreign Policy: A Bureaucratic Perspective*. Boston, MA: Little, Brown, pp. 98–110.

Time Magazine. (2022). Biden: US would defend Taiwan from "unprecedented attack." September 18. https://time.com/6214511/biden-defend-taiwan-china-us/.

Toal, G. (2017). *Near Abroad: Putin, the West, and the Contest over Ukraine and the Caucasus*. Oxford: Oxford University Press.

Trachtenberg, M. (2007). Preventive war and U.S. foreign policy. *Security Studies*, 16(1), 1–31.

Trachtenberg, M. (2012). Audience costs: An historical analysis. *Security Studies*, 21(1), 3–42.

Treisman, D. (2004). Rational appeasement. *International Organization*, 58(2), 344–73.

Tyler, P. (1999). *A Great Wall, Six Presidents and China: An Investigative History*. New York: Perseus.

Van Evera, S. (1984). The cult of offensive and the origins of the First World War. *International Security*, 9(1), 58–107.

Van Evera, S. (1999). *Causes of War: Power and the Roots of Conflict*. Ithaca, NY: Cornell University Press.

Vasquez, J. A. (1993). *The War Puzzle*. Cambridge: Cambridge University Press.

Vasquez, J. A. (2009). Whether and how global leadership transitions will result in war: Some long-term predictions from steps-to-war explanation. In W. R. Thompson, ed., *Systemic Transitions: Past, Present, and Future*. New York: Palgrave Macmillan, pp. 131–60.

References

Vogel, E. F. (1979). *Japan as Number One: Lessons for America*. Cambridge, MA: Harvard University Press.

Wachman, A. M. (2007). *Why Taiwan: Geostrategic Rationales for China's Territorial Integrity*. Stanford, CA: Stanford University Press.

Walt, S. M. (2005). *Taming American Power: The Global Response to U.S. Primacy*. New York: Norton.

Waltz, K. N. (1979). *Theory of International Politics*. Reading, MA: Addison-Wesley.

Wang, T. Y. (2017). Changing boundaries: The development of the Taiwan voters' identity. In C. H. Achen and T. Y. Wang, eds., *The Taiwan Voter*. Ann Arbor, MI: University of Michigan Press, pp. 45–70.

Wang, T. Y. (2021). Strategic Ambiguity or Strategic Clarity? US Policy toward the Taiwan Issue. *Taiwan Insight*. June 7. https://taiwaninsight.org/2021/06/07/strategic-ambiguity-or-strategic-clarity-us-policy-towards-the-taiwan-issue/.

Wang, T. Y. & Cheng, S. F. (2024). Strategic clarity and Taiwanese citizens' confidence in the US security commitment. *Asian Survey*, 64(1), 54–78.

Wang, T. Y. & Liu, I. C. (2004). Contending identities in Taiwan: Implications for cross-Strait relations. *Asian Survey*, 44(4), 568–90.

Ward, S. (2017). *Status and the Challenge of Rising Powers*. Cambridge: Cambridge University Press.

Wayman, F., Singer, J. D. & Goertz, G. (1983). Capabilities, allocations, and success in militarized disputes and wars, 1816–1976. *International Studies Quarterly*, 27(4), 497–515.

Welch, D. (2015). Can the United States and China avoid a Thucydides Trap? E-International relations. www.e-ir.info/2015/04/06/can-the-united-states-and-china-avoid-a-thucydides-trap/.

Welch, D. (2020). China, the United States, and the "Thucydides's Trap." In H. Feng and K. He, eds., *China's Challenges and International Order Transition: Beyond "Thucydides's Trap."* Ann Arbor, MI: University of Michigan Press, pp. 47–70.

Wendt, A. (1992). Anarchy is what states make of it: The social construction of power politics. *International Organization*, 46(2), 391–425.

The White House. (2002). *The National Security Strategy of the United States of America*. U.S. State Department. https://2009-2017.state.gov/documents/organization/63562.pdf.

Whiting, A. S. (1962). *China Crosses the Yalu: The Decision to Enter the Korean War*. Stanford, CA: Stanford University Press.

Whiting, A. S. (1975). *The Chinese Calculus of Deterrence: India and Indochina*. Ann Arbor, MI: University of Michigan Press.

References

Wildavsky, A. (1964). *The Politics of the Budgetary Process*. Boston, MA: Little, Brown.

Wildavsky, A. (1975). *Budgeting: A Comparative Theory of Budgetary Process*. Boston, MA: Little, Brown.

Wingrove, J. (2022). Biden says US would defend Taiwan in "Unprecedented Attack." *Bloomberg*, September 18. www.bloomberg.com/news/articles/2022-09-18/biden-says-us-would-defend-taiwan-from-unprecedented-attack.

Wohlstetter, R. (1962). *Pearl Harbor: Warning and Decision*. Stanford, CA: Stanford University Press.

Wolf, R. (2014). Rising powers, status ambitions, and the need to reassure: What China could learn from imperial Germany's failures. *Chinese Journal of International Politics* 7(2), 185–219.

Woodward, B. & Costa, R. (2021). *Peril*. New York: Simon & Schuster.

Wu, Y-S. (2016). Heading towards troubled waters? The impact of Taiwan's 2016 elections on cross-Strait Relations. *American Journal of Chinese Studies*, 23(1), 59–75.

Yang, Z. (2016). Explaining national identity shift in Taiwan. *Journal of Contemporary China*, 25(99), 336–52.

Zakaria, F. (2020). The new China scare: Why America shouldn't panic about its latest challenger. *Foreign Affairs*, 99(1), 52–69.

Zakaria, F. (2024). Opinion: the world's most dangerous place has only gotten even more dangerous. *Cable News Network (CNN)*, March 10. www.cnn .com/2024/03/10/opinions/taiwan-china-us-tensions-war-zakaria/index. html.

Zelleke, A. (2020). "Strategic clarity" won't solve the United States' Taiwan dilemma: An open commitment to defend Taiwan won't mean much unless the U.S. has the certain capacity to do so. *The Diplomat*, October 2. https:// thediplomat.com/2020/10/strategic-clarity-wont-solve-the-united-states-tai wan-dilemma/.

Zhang, K. (2024). *China's Gambit: The Calculus of Coercion*. Cambridge: Cambridge University Press.

Acknowledgments

I thank two anonymous reviewers for their constructive feedback. Their suggestions and advice have encouraged me to clarify, sharpen, and expand on my arguments, for which I am grateful. I am especially indebted to one of the reviewers whose observations are incorporated in my summation of Section 1.

Cambridge Elements ≡

Indo-Pacific Security

Kai He
Griffith University

Kai He is Professor of International Relations at Griffith University, Australia. He has authored or co-authored six books and edited or co-edited six volumes. Among his notable works are *Institutional Balancing in the Asia Pacific* (Routledge, 2009), *China's Crisis Behavior: Political Survival and Foreign Policy* (Cambridge, 2016), and *After Hedging* (Cambridge Elements in International Relations in 2023).

Steve Chan
University of Colorado Boulder

Steve Chan is College Professor of Distinction (Emeritus) at the University of Colorado Boulder. His publications include twenty-five books and about two hundred articles and chapters. His most recent book is *Culture, Economic Growth, and Interstate Power Shift: Implications for Competition between China and the United States* (Cambridge University Press, 2024).

Rumi Aoyama
Waseda University

Rumi Aoyama is Professor at the Graduate School of Asia-Pacific Studies at Waseda University and Director of Waseda Institute of Contemporary Chinese Studies. Her publications include thirteen books and more than one hundred and fifty articles and chapters. Her book *Contemporary China's Foreign Policy*[Gendai chuugoku no gaikou] was honored with the 24th Masayoshi Ohira Foundation Memorial Prize.

Advisory Board

Amitav Acharya, *American University*
Dewi Fortuna Anwar, *National Research and Innovation Agency (BRIN), Indonesia*
Mely Caballero-Anthony, *Nanyang Technological University*
Rosemary Foot, *University of Oxford*
Evelyn Goh, *Australian National University*
Deborah Larson, *University of California, Los Angeles*
T.V. Paul, *McGill University*
Yan Xuetong, *Tsinghua University*

About the Series

Elements in Indo-Pacific Security publishes original and authoritative works on diverse security topics, encompassing not only traditional issues of war and peace but also emerging concerns such as space competition and climate change. It also explores interactions among actors within this region and between them and others beyond it.

Cambridge Elements ≡

Indo-Pacific Security

Elements in the Series

Taiwan and the Danger of a Sino-American War
Steve Chan

A full series listing is available at: www.cambridge.org/EIPS

www.ingramcontent.com/pod-product-compliance
Ingram Content Group UK Ltd.
Pitfield, Milton Keynes, MK11 3LW, UK
UKHW020634030125
452982UK00012B/91